Tales of Old Jamaica

Tales of
Old Jamaica

CLINTON V. BLACK F.S.A.

Longman Caribbean

Longman Group UK Limited
Longman House, Burnt Mill, Harlow
Essex CM20 2JE, England
and Associated Companies throughout the world

Longman Jamaica Limited
PO Box 489
43 Second Street
Newport West
Kingston 10
Jamaica

Longman Caribbean (Trinidad) Limited
Boundary Road
San Juan
Trinidad

This edition first published by Collins Educational 1983
This impression published by Longman Group UK Ltd 1988

Produced by Longman Group (FE) Ltd
Printed in Hong Kong

ISBN 0 582 03897 9

Contents

Foreword   *page* 7

Annee Palmer of Rose Hall   11

The Man who was Buried Twice   27

The Golden Table   33

The Mission that Failed   53

The Women Pirates   62

The Mad Master of Edinburgh Castle   78

Mistress of the Jamaican Revels   89

The Case of the Counterfeit Doubloons   100

Three-fingered Jack   110

The Shark Papers   120

Acknowledgements   128

Illustrations

Rose Hall Estate, from *A Picturesque Tour of the Island of Jamaica* .... by James Hakewill. London, 1825   *page* 11

Broadside of the Port Royal earthquake of 1692   27

The Square, Spanish Town (St. Jago de la Vega) from *The History of Jamaica* by Edward Long. London, 1774   33

General Robert Venables, from a contemporary portrait, artist unknown   53

Anne Bonney and Mary Read, from *A General History of the Pirates* by Captain Charles Johnson. First published 1724   62

The King against Lewis Hutchison. *Pleas of the Crown* 1770-1783   78

Teresa Constantia Phillips, from the painting by John Highmore which accompanies her *Apology*. London, 1748   89

Kingston Parish Church, from *Daguerian Excursions in Jamaica* .... by Adolphe Duperly. Kingston, Ja. 1844   100

The death of Three-fingered Jack, from *The Wonderful Life and Adventures of Three-Fingered Jack.* ..... London, 1829   110

Kingston Court House, from *Daguerian Excursions in Jamaica* .... by Adolphe Duperly. Kingston, Ja. 1844   120

Foreword

JAMAICA, largest of the former British West Indian islands, lies some ninety miles due south of Cuba and the same distance west of Haiti. The island is fortunate in the richness of its history and in the surviving documentary sources for that history.

Discovered by Columbus in 1494 while on his second voyage to the New World, more than fifteen years were to pass before an attempt was made to colonise it. The Spaniards were disappointed in the country's lack of gold, and Jamaica became a neglected appanage of the Columbus family, poor and sparsely populated. Its chief value to Spain was as a supply base, the main occupation of its settlers cattle-ranching.

In 1655 the island fell to an invasion force sent out by Oliver Cromwell as part of his plan aimed against Spain known as the "Western Design." The first colony in the Americas to be captured by a formal British expedition, Jamaica became also the first of Britain's West Indian possessions to achieve independence.

The aboriginal inhabitants, the peaceful Arawak Indians, had been exterminated before the British arrived and the importation of African slave labour, begun by the Spaniards, continued under the new regime, growing steadily in volume as sugar production grew in extent and value, until by the eighteenth-century hey-day Jamaica, and the other "sugar colonies," had become the most valuable possessions of any empire, fiercely fought over in every war that broke out in Europe and as fiercely bargained for at every peace conference.

The abolition of the slave trade in 1807 and full emancipation thirty-one years later caused the collapse of the plantation system. This, together with other factors, produced a crisis in 1865 which changed for all time the old social and economic patterns.

The story of the island's recovery and development, social, constitutional and economic during the succeeding hundred years, and its evolution into the sovereign state of to-day, is the stirring story of the new Jamaica.

It is against this background that the tales here told are set. They do not, of course, cover the island's history. Such is not their purpose. But in them the reader will find illuminated many periods of that history and many significant events, beginning with the capture of the island in 1655.

These tales vary in nature. They are not folk tales, although folk-lore obtrudes itself here and there, and one story—that of *The Golden Table*—has as its basis a Jamaican legend with the distinguishing ring of authentic tradition about it.

Nor are these fictional stories, although here and there I have allowed myself the liberty of "imagining the motives and modes of passion that influenced the characters" who figure in them. For the most part these are true stories. In spite of the studied absence of footnotes, appendices and the like, most are matters of history and their composition has led through libraries abroad as well as the Jamaica Institute's West India Reference section, through overseas record collections as well as the Jamaica Archives. It was in these Jamaica Archives that most of the new information which I have been fortunate enough to bring to these tales has been discovered. The most valuable perhaps of these discoveries was that of the identity (hitherto unknown or wrongly guessed at) of the Kingston clergyman in *The Case of the Counterfeit Doubloons*. The story as given here is, in fact, largely a study in detection. The most revolutionary perhaps of these discoveries concerned the case of Lewis Hutchison, *The Mad Master of Edinburgh Castle*. The previously accepted version of this story made Hutchison out to be the only actor in the grim drama (except for his mutely submissive slaves) whereas the details of his trial discovered in the records of the Jamaica Grand Court reveal that he had gathered around him a cast of perverts in some respects as vicious as himself. The Rev. Bridges whose recital of his "dark and midnight crimes" had hitherto supplied us with our chief source for this story, is said to have obtained his information from the slaves of the district as it was current at the time. Did the clergyman-historian report them faithfully? And had the memory of Hutchison by then quite usurped that of his partners in crime?

We must take one man's word for the not unreasonable account of *The Mission that Failed*, while in marked contrast the story of *The Shark Papers*—one of the most unusual in legal history, a story in fact which points the adage that truth is stranger than fiction—is authentic and documented at every turn.

The story of *Annee Palmer of Rose Hall*, the story of a sinister beauty of debauched habits noted for cruelty to her slaves and the murder of husbands and lovers, is in a class by itself. Careful research over the last couple of years by my friend and colleague Geoffrey S. Yates has failed to produce any evidence to support this reputation for cruelty or the commonly held tales of luxury and lovers. In his paper "The Death of a Legend", published in the Jamaican newspaper *The Daily Gleaner* of 21st November and 6th December 1965, Mr. Yates has ably stated his case and furnished the fruits of his researches in support. But the Rose Hall legend is of sturdy growth and shows no sign of wilting. Already the subject of a successful novel, a film is now to be made of the story; it is planned to develop part of the estate as a private residential property and the coastal area as a tourist resort, while costly restoration work on the great house itself is almost complete.

The *Old Jamaica* of the title means Jamaica during the first two centuries or so of British rule, from the expedition of 1655 which captured the island from the Spaniards to the last days of plantation slavery, with a faint, distant rumble of the earthquake of 1907 that shook the city of Kingston to the ground and added one short episode to the curious case of *The Shark Papers*.

Foreword

As these stories range in time so they do in space—from Plymouth England, to the American port of Baltimore, from seventeenth-century Flanders to the buccaneer rendezvous of New Providence in the Bahamas, from Breda to Hispaniola, from Carolina to Curacao.

C.V.B.

1966

Rose Hall Estate

Annee Palmer of Rose Hall

EVEN NOW it seems strange to think of Annee Palmer dead; strange and difficult too it must have been even for the intelligent white planters to do so at the time, and no doubt, for long after; for her own slaves and those on the neighbouring plantations it would have been impossible. To them she probably *was* and always would be—this white woman with all the black powers of witchcraft and obeah behind her, this creature of evil, who could, and often did, dispense with equal ease the gifts of life and death, must herself have had no commencement and no ending.

Even when in terrified silence they filed on soft, bare feet into the room to stare at the frail and faded body of their mistress flung untidily across the bed with awful open eyes and strangled throat, they could not have believed that she was really dead. Her body was lifeless. That they knew. But that did not necessarily mean the end of Annee Palmer.

So, open-mouthed they passed noiselessly in and out of the room, but never touched the thing on the bed. Nor could they be induced to do so. Finally the neighbouring planters came, led by Samuel Moulton-Barrett, uncle of Elizabeth Browning, braced by tall glasses of their own old rum for the task they relished less than did the slaves. By soft means and harsh, with promises of gifts and now and then a cut from riding crop and buggy whip they urged their grooms and coachmen to help with the burial.

For Annee Palmer was dead, blast it!—strangled dead. By whom? Who gave a damn?—slave, paramour—who knew, who cared? It should have happened long ago. Bury the slut, do anything, only hurry; let's get it over with and let's get out of this foul room. Throw something over her damn' staring eyes and fling her in a hole, anywhere, so long as you dig it deep—here, here in the centre of the garden, by the east wing of the great house, here in the sunset shadow of her own Rose Hall.

They got a man at length to do the thing, a Negro mason named Downer from Sam Barrett's Cinnamon Hill, and over the spot he built a plain square pile of solid masonry two feet thick, the mortar mixed with ash from the burnt-out cane-fields fired some time before by the outraged slaves. They offered him silver for his pains, but he refused it. Instead he took a young bull calf and went his way with the years.

So Annee Palmer died—at least, so it is said—and was buried at Rose Hall and not in the church of St. James ten miles farther down the coast as some contend. The lovely monument by John Bacon one sees there is to another Mrs. Palmer, a good and virtuous Mrs. Rosa Palmer who died on the 1st of May, 1790. "Her manners were open," says her epitaph, "cheerful and agreeable and being blessed with a plentiful fortune hospitality dwelt with her as long as health permitted her to enjoy society. Educated by the anxious care of a Reverend Divine, her father, her charities were not ostentatious but of a nobler kind. She was warm in her attachment to her friends and gave the most signal proof of it in the last moments of her life. This tribute of affection and respect is erected by her husband the Honourable John Palmer as a monument of her worth and of his gratitude."

A very different person this from the later mistress of Rose Hall whose death—they say—took place some forty-three years after. And yet their histories are in some respects connected, as we shall see.

For our purposes Rosa's story began on 16th July, 1746, with her marriage to a certain Henry Fanning of the parish of St. Catherine. Rich and prosperous, with the pleasing prospect of a satisfactory union, Fanning set out on a tour of the island to find the ideal situation for the great mansion he had carried in his mind for many years. His first glimpse of the spot that was to become the Rose Hall site was sufficient to decide him in its favour. Money was no object and in the January of the same year he bought the property with its 300 acres of caneland and its long stretch of lovely coastline for £3,000. Six months later he married the "agreeable" Rosa Kelly. But life was short in the Jamaica of those days: in another six months he was dead, with his hopes and plans for the home he always yearned for still largely unfulfilled, leaving to his "dearest and best beloved wife" almost the whole of his large fortune.

Four years later Rosa Fanning married her second husband, a planter of St. James named George Ash. Two years were all they were to have together for Ash died in 1752, but in those two years he had carried the plans of Henry Fanning to fruition and saw, before he died, the splendid white stone great house rise in all its majesty against the dark green foothills of the coastal range.

It is very difficult in these days of altered values to imagine the magnificence of a planter's home which at that time could cost—as Rose Hall did—as much as £30,000 to build. James Hakewill the artist and architect who visited Jamaica in 1820 /21 and saw the place at the height of its glory, wrote: "The house is justly considered as the best in Jamaica. It is placed at a delightful elevation and commands a very extensive sea view. Its general appearance has much of the character of a handsome Italian villa. A double flight of stone steps leads to an open portico, giving access to the entrance hall; on the left of which is the eating-room, and on the right the drawing-room, behind which are other apartments for domestic uses. The right wing, fitted up with great elegance, and enriched with painting and gilding, was the private apartment of the late Mrs. Palmer, and the left wing is occupied as servants' apartments and offices. The principal staircase, in the body of the house, is a specimen of joinery in mahogany and other costly woods seldom excelled, and leads to a suite of chambers in the upper story."

Of interest also is this brief account by a Scottish clergyman who knew the house after its glory had passed, having "preached in the large hall of that building, fit to receive 200 people" on the first three Sundays of August, 1830: "Though unoccupied, save by rats, bats, and owls, it had once been a specimen of the fine colonial mansions of the island aristocracy, when West Indian proprietors were like an order of nobility . . . Its floors and stairs, wainscoting and ceiling, doors and windows, were of mahogany, cedar, rosewood, ebony, orange, and other native hardwoods of various colours, fit for cabinet-work, highly polished and well arranged. Spacious piazzas and corridors ran around the house above and below, and the front door was reached by a very elegant double flight of stone steps."

To this mansion then, writes Joseph Shore in his book of parish chronicles, made beautiful with furniture and ornaments in accord with its grandeur and fittings, its galleries and staircase hung with the family portraits in oils, its library stored to meet the intellectual demands of its mistress, its music-room in the great east wing, ever ready to ring to spinet or to song—to this mansion then the Honourable Norwood Witter of Westmoreland, a widower and a gallant, came a-courting early in "crop-time" of 1753. "But here, for once, the heart of Rosa Kelly misled her. Norwood Witter, whom she married in May—oh! unlucky May bride— thought more of her fortune than of her happiness, and the course of married life for the next thirteen years as a consequence did not run very smoothly. The Honourable Norwood made frequent calls upon her purse, the strings of which ran all too easily on the rings. Yet though hers was not the temperament, as we well know, to be either close-fisted or mean, she keenly resented the demands made at 'sundry times' for large sums to keep her husband's head above water."

His death in 1765 brought her no grief, but not so the passing of her father, the Reverend John Kelly, Rector of St. Elizabeth, the following year. This came as a heavy blow to Rosa for she loved him dearly. A good clergyman and an excellent father, he had given her "an education beyond the usual and a friendship deeper than is the custom of most fathers."

But these were the *Christmas Northers* of her life, as they say on the north coast; the rest was to prove a peaceful crop-time. At the age of forty-five she married her fourth husband, the Honourable John Palmer, Custos of St. James, a man of wealth and position and the owner of neighbouring Palmyra estate, with whom she was to spend more than a score of happy years, and to whom by her will she left all the residue of her vast estate, real and personal, he being "most deserving thereof." In love and gratitude John Palmer commissioned that handsome marble monument, carved by the great John Bacon himself, which stands to this day in the parish church of St. James, some ten miles down the coast.

And there we leave the good and virtuous lady for there her story ends and, for our purposes, that of the *other* Mrs. Palmer begins. Two years later the Honourable John "having proved himself a faithful husband to two wives, and being himself of an affectionate temperament," found Rose Hall rather a cheerless place, in spite of its magnificence, and so married a twenty-year-old maiden, Rebecca James. But, says the chronicler, "he did not survive long to enjoy the solace which his young wife presumably brought him." He died on the 19th March, 1797, and that night a shadow fell across the great house.

Oddly enough John Palmer did not leave the two properties Rose Hall and Palmyra to his young widow. Indeed, two months after his death she packed her bags and left for England, never to return. Under his will (as, in fact, they had been under his marriage settlement) both properties were placed in trust and, instead of a dower, he settled on his widow an annuity of £2,800 Jamaica currency to be paid out of the profits of the plantations which were to be held to the use of the children of his then present wife; there being none, to the use of his sons by his first wife, John and James, and the survivors of them and their heirs successively. Both lived in England, never visited Jamaica and died childless. By the terms of their father's will, therefore, the properties reverted to the eldest or other son of his nephew James Palmer and his heirs in fee. That son—grand-nephew of the Honourable John—a young man of fashion and taste, was John Rose Palmer.

With as little delay as possible the young heir settled his affairs in England and sailed for Jamaica to take up his inheritance. But there was much for the new master to do. For twenty years the Rose Hall great house had been closed and shuttered. It stood in need of repair as did also Palmyra. Furniture too was needed since, in addition to the handsome annuity, John Palmer had bequeathed his widow certain slaves and silver as well as a pianoforte and sundry other items of personal property.

John Rose lost no time and spared no expense in restoring the mansion to its former glory. Carpenters, cabinet-makers, masons, painters, all were put to work on the house, and field gangs turned out to clean up the pasture through which the carriage-drive ran. The drive itself had to be repaired with stone for the base and many ox-cart loads of marl for surface dressing. It took the carpenters a fortnight to re-roof one of the great house wings with shingles especially ordered from Montego Bay and not split on the estate, as was the custom, from the fragrant, seasoned cedar wood the property so lavishly produced.

The affairs of the estates themselves demanded attention. It was imperative for both to turn over a high and sustained profit since the heavy annuity had to be paid before the extravagant John could touch a penny. And how quickly the time for payment seemed to come around. How quickly time seemed to pass in this strange country of eternal summer! A single summer—so it seemed—but twelve full months had passed, twelve busy fruitful months, and now it was late December of the year 1819, as John one day reined in his horse at the massive gateway to the property, the gateposts standing twice his own height. In the distance stood the great house, restored, repainted, fresh and glorious in the soft December sunlight. And he was satisfied, this young man of fashion and taste, for all things now were ready. On the 28th of March, 1820, the richly carven doors swung open on their huge brass hinges to admit the new master of Rose Hall and his beautiful but haughty bride, Annee Mary Paterson.

Annee, who was barely seventeen at the time of her marriage, was the only child of John Paterson of The Baulk—a property near Lucea in the parish of Hanover—and Juliana his wife. The early writers, jealous of their details, tell us little about the new mistress of Rose Hall except that she was beautiful and proud. But she was other things as well, as we shall see. She was restless, ambitious, dark-tempered and strong-willed, but above all she was dissatisfied—in marked contrast to her husband who was so well pleased with almost everything. Always, when the opportunity afforded, he would pause at the great gateway to the estate and gaze with pride and admiration at his mansion, his magnificent Rose Hall. But it was otherwise with Annee Palmer. Sensitive as she was to atmosphere, the house itself had had a bad effect upon her from the moment she had entered it. Perhaps its unaccustomed splendour made her uneasy and unsure; perhaps the ghosts of the past still haunted its vast rooms, mocking at her unease, her unhappiness; or perhaps she had seen the shadow that rested on the place despite its gilt and polish. So, in the rich house she brooded, restless, eager, but above all dissatisfied.

It was some time after their marriage and only by merest chance that John Palmer found out about his wife's affair with the young slave. In his great anger he was terrible, almost magnificent. If he had shown such spirit before, matters might have turned out differently, she told herself: but now it was too late. She could forget the humiliation and the red weals his riding crop had raised, but what really terrified was the realisation that John Palmer had found himself, and who could say where that would end? She would certainly never see her lover again and she would certainly never be mistress in Rose Hall again.

John Palmer usually took a glass of wine before he retired to bed. That night one glass was not enough, but he was far from drunk by the time he finally rose and yet his legs would scarcely bear him. He barely reached his room when he collapsed on the bed clutching his stomach in awful agony. Suddenly Annee was standing at the door, bare footed and thinly clad, her black hair hanging down across her shoulders. Behind her, almost filling the doorway, stood the massive, half-dressed figure of the young slave. She laughed, softly, mockingly at first, then her voice rose, high-pitched and half-hysterical. From the bed John Palmer stared with pain-crazed eyes at his wife. The poison was strong, already he could barely move a limb and his breath came in gasps. In thick and heavy accents he cursed her and, summoning the little strength he had, cried out despairingly for help. Annee's laughter died on her lips. What if someone in the house should hear his cries, his curses!

"Kill him!" she told the slave, "stop his mouth, I can't bear to hear his voice!—here, do it with the pillow."

It was over very quickly, and soon Annee Palmer was laughing again, high-pitched and half-hysterical.

When she woke the following morning a sudden, cold panic swept over her. In the bedroom her husband lay dead. Beside her was the lover for whom she had done the deed. Arrangements had to be made about the murdered John, his death somehow explained, his burial seen to. She must think these things out carefully and quickly. How she coped we will never know, but cope she did, and successfully too. John Rose Palmer was given Christian burial on the 5th November, 1827, the ceremony being performed by the curate, a Reverend J. Smith. As the Parish Register shows, he was forty-two years old.

So Annee Palmer had coped successfully. John had been removed from the scene and the method of his removal effectively concealed. But was that really so? Would he and the crime itself not always haunt her as long as her lover lived? For *he* knew her secret. He only. None knew it better than he. She was in his power, as long as he lived. This was the spectre that now leered at her from the dark corners of the house, this the fear that followed her night and day . . . as long as he lived.

She was present the day they did it. The day they flogged him to death, securely tied and gagged. She sat on her tall black horse ten yards away and watched until it was over. It lasted long, for he was young. But the gag had been well fixed. No word escaped his lips and even his cries were scarcely audible. One of the young, white book-keepers stood by her side, holding her horse's head, until it was over. That night he dined at the great house. That night Annee Palmer took more wine that was her custom and chatted more loudly and nervously than she generally did. For the spectre was gone from the dark corners, but the old dissatisfaction had returned, the nameless yearning which the young book-keeper failed to satisfy.

With John Rose out of the way and Annee in full charge of the two properties, a change took place in the estate management. All day now from across the canefields came the sound of the lash and the ceaseless, savage cry of the drivers, "Work! Work!"

To her critics Annee excused the harshness of Rose Hall life on the ground that only with the aid of the cart-whip could the property make the forced crops one after another which were necessary if the heavy annuity, paid each year from out the profits, could be met. But this did not save Rose Hall from the stigma of a *bad* estate, and in the Bay, ten miles down the coast, there was much ugly talk about the place and its mistress, for it was becoming increasingly clear, from the rumours that had seeped out, that much of this cruelty was not in the way of business, but had become in a measure a perverted satisfaction for this appalling woman "hardened now beyond ordinary delights."

From nearby Cornwall estate came a Scottish missionary once. His stay was short, for his visit was not welcomed. But, before he left he saw the spikes and iron collars, the stocks and flogging posts. He did not see the cellars under the great house, nor sit in on a session there, but before he left he saw the wild and terrible look in the eyes of the Rose Hall slaves. It was enough.

Fear like a foul, chill fog hung over the estate. In his small thatched hut even Old Jack, the village obeahman, shook from the cold touch of it. The slaves had come to him for help and he had promised it. But now he was afraid. And not without reason. For Annee Palmer was no ordinary white woman. Strange things were done at the great house, strange evil things which made even Old Jack shake to think about, for he feared her power and her witchcraft learnt, they said, in voodoo-ridden Haiti. What if his plan should be revealed to her? What if her obeah proved too strong for his? What was that dog he had seen last night, that huge black dog that slunk across the narrow bridle path, its eyes glowing red and malevolent in the darkness, then vanished in the thick bush? What were those hoof-beats going down the hill? A horse perhaps, a horse whose rider sat backwards in the saddle, sat and stared at Old Jack's hut, at a wall of the hut, at a small nail hole in the wall where soon that rider would press two full red lips to suck the startled soul from his body! Such things, such evil things were done. And Old Jack was afraid, for the slaves had come to him for help and he had promised it.

If he were to help them—(God help himself!)—he must make sure as *she* herself had done that night her husband died. For that he needed someone else's help, someone with access to the great house, someone perhaps like Princess who could put the white powder in the glass of milk her mistress drank each day about eleven . . .

That morning, busier than usual writing letters, Annee Palmer left her milk untouched for nearly an hour before remembering it. She had almost raised the rummer to her lips when she saw the sediment, thick and chalklike, at the bottom of the glass. She put the milk down and without comment sent immediately for her doctor. His analysis was brief: the sediment was deadly poison.

When the news reached the slave yard Old Jack was seen to drop his hoe and run like a madman into the fields. They caught him eventually, but by then he had disposed of the fistful of white powder he had been carrying in his trouser pocket. In the meantime Princess and the great house cook had both been put under arrest, all three being later sent on to Montego Bay for trial at the next sitting of the court. For once the summary justice of Rose Hall was suspended, for the doctor had gossiped and too many outsiders now knew about the incident.

At the hearing almost all the house Negroes, wide-eyed with fear, were placed on the witness-stand, but Mrs. Palmer herself gave the chief evidence. The case against the cook and the obeahman was soon dismissed, and for a time it seemed as though Princess herself might be acquitted for no one had seen her mix the poison with the milk. But, in the end, the weight of evidence went against her: she was convicted and condemned to death.

Outside the court house Annee Palmer received the congratulations of the few people who for one reason or another were still on speaking terms with her, without warmth or enthusiasm.

"It matters little how the case has turned out," she said grimly, "for if my slave had a thousand lives, I would have taken them all!"

As soon as judgment was pronounced she asked that the head of the woman be delivered to her after the execution. To Old Jack she gave the job of collecting the ghastly, bleeding thing and carrying it home in a basket. Hardened slave and obeahman though he was, the task proved too much for him, and the head—proud trophy of the white woman's victory over the African's witchcraft—would not have reached Rose Hall if the young butler-boy had not carried the dripping basket for much of the dreadful ten-mile journey by dismal mangrove swamp and lonely canefield.

Stuck on the sharpened end of a slender bamboo pole, the head was placed above the corn house, a short distance from the great house itself, where in the fierce heat it festered and decayed, as did all hope in the hearts of those who saw it.

Even when John Rose Palmer had been alive Annee had had little contact with the neighbouring planter families—the Barretts and the Lawrences, the Scarletts, Goodins and the rest. But now the events of the last few years following her husband's death had closed for good the doors of Rose Hall to them.

Shunned, despised and feared, she spent almost all her time on the property, a prey to the terrible gusts of passion and the nameless yearning which nothing seemed to satisfy. She took to drink: perhaps to drown the stings of remorse, suggests the chronicler. "Her nights were spent amid drunken orgies," he tells us, "scenes too disgusting to describe, while her days were spent in inflicting the most tyrannical cruelties and dreadful tortures upon her slaves, who were alternately the companions of her evening orgies and the victims of her morning remorse."

One of her favourite pastimes was to get into male clothes and ride round the property at night, hunting for stray or philandering slaves who, when caught, were beaten brutally. When staying at Palmyra, as she often did, she frequently descended on Rose Hall by the old bridle track through Music Valley on the lookout for any of her slaves who, counting on her absence, were unwise enough as to go beyond the village limits.

The incident with Princess and the poison had confirmed the belief that she could command the powers of black magic for her purposes, a belief which she did nothing to remove. It was this fear of her dread power alone that saved her when on December 27th, 1831, the outraged slaves at Palmyra, a hundred and seven strong, set the canepieces afire, for in the great house Annee Palmer sat alone, except for her two constant companions, a sambo boy of thirteen and a sixteen-year-old mulatto girl.

Feared and hated by her slaves, shunned and avoided by the people of her own class, she turned more and more to the colony of white, unmarried book-keepers on the property for companionship and the satisfaction she was never to find. "Here to hand, then, were her subjects," says the chronicler, "and with them the grossly dissolute mistress of Rose Hall, as the tradition of the neighbourhood declares her to have been, contracted liaison after liaison, drawing victim after victim into the toils. Such stories as have been told by Rose Hall house servants and their descendants show that some of these persons with whom she formed illicit connections met an untimely end. Poison was put forward as the chief means employed, but the cause of death given to the world was usually a dangerous fever.

"In any event," he continues, "a life led, as it was latterly, in the seclusion of a hill-engirdled estate, far from the beaten track, and under the indifferent observation of a boy and a girl slave, was not at all likely to attract notice or evoke gossip. But there is still another point. The sudden death of these young men while holding intercourse with Mrs. Palmer was not at all likely to excite suspicion. It is a notorious fact that not less than 90 per cent. of the young men who in those days came to the colony to work on the estates died off from the effects of fever, of fast living, and hard drinking. . . How many men thus met their fate through these intrigues is not definitely known, but the general impression gathered from tradition is that there were several."

But more than tradition survived until well into remembered times. On the floor of the north front bedroom bordering on the western side of the passage leading to the upper balcony, the blood of one of Annee Palmer's murdered playthings could, until the house fell into ruin, be clearly seen. His story was little different from the others, only he left grim evidence behind. She had grown tired of him, as she had done of those before him. She had already lighted on her new lover. The old one had to go. One night, as he entered her bedroom, a strong black arm came out of the darkness and encircled his neck; his single cry ended in a coughing sob as the knife was driven hard between his shoulder blades. The larger bloodstain marked the place where he fell, the other showed the neat and shapely form of a woman's foot, the naked foot of Annee Palmer.

But here, for once, events turned out strangely. The new lover on whom she had set her heart—the white cooper for the estate, a handsome, coarse, unlettered brute of a man, with passions as fierce and temper as fiery as her own—proved impervious to her charms and blandishments. This was a new, exciting experience for the woman who had always had her way. She tried the many, time-tested lures she knew, from the coy and timid invitation to the stern, imperious message of command, but all to no purpose. It seemed that the cooper never had time for anything but work; his services were always in demand, mostly at Palmyra, super-intending the splitting of staves for sugar hogsheads, and a thousand other matters—or so he said. Meanwhile at the great house Annee Palmer ached with the humiliation and delay, and in the book-keepers' quarters and even down in the Bay the big white cooper boasted openly of his achievement.

But there is always a way and Annee Palmer was the one to find it. One morning while riding over to Palmyra the cooper was surprised to meet his employer travelling along the road also, out (as she declared) for an early morning canter. She was riding her favourite black stallion, a superb creature, full of zest and spirit. It was as much as she could do to hold him to the cooper's slow pace and when he slipped on a smooth flat stone, once common enough on that road, she lost control completely. The horse bolted with Annee hanging sidewards in her saddle from which she was soon thrown as the stallion broke into a gallop. She tumbled headforemost, her dress and underclothes billowing up around her waist leaving her considerably exposed and, in the words of another writer, revealing limbs of an exquisite symmetry which (being per-haps too giddy and upset) she made no effort to conceal. With bulging eyes the cooper rode quickly up and dismounted beside her. Delicacy, says our friend the chronicler, renders impossible a literal transcript of the conversation which followed.

At length the cooper rose, hurriedly remounted his horse and rode off at a savage pace towards Palmyra. Annee Palmer watched him out of sight, laughing grimly, for now he would come to Rose Hall, to-night he would come and she would be ready to receive him.

The next day she was dead—at least, so it is said. Strangled dead. By whom? Who gave a damn?—slave, paramour, who knew, who cared? It should have happened long ago, they said, as they dug her grave in the centre of the garden, by the east wing of the great house, in the sunset shadow of her own Rose Hall.

But it seems strange, even now, to think of Annee Palmer dead. Rose Hall, as she knew it, is gone. Relatively little remains to-day of the house that was once the finest in Jamaica. Its furnishings and fittings have rotted or been removed. The handsome staircase, the wide verandas and fine porticoes have disappeared and the two great wings have gone with the wind from the open sea that rushes like the restless soul of the mistress herself through the empty doors and casements of Rose Hall.

A True and Perfect Relation of that most Sad and Terrible

EARTHQUAKE, at Port-Royal in JAMAICA,

Which happened on *Tuesday* the 7th. of *June*, 1692.

Where, in Two Minutes time the Town was Sunk under Ground, and Two Thousand Souls Perished; With the manner of it at Large; in a Letter from thence, Written by Captain *Crocker*: As also of the *Earthquake* which happen'd in *England, Holland, Flanders, France, Germany, Zealand, &c.* And in most Parts of *Europe*: On *Thursday* the 8th of *September*. Being a Dreadful Warning to the Sleepy World: Or, God's heavy Judgments shewd on a Sinful People, as a Fore-runner of the Terrible Day of the Lord.

Broadside of the Port Royal earthquake of 1692

The Man who was Buried Twice

THERE CAN be few places in the world with a more colourful and romantic past than Port Royal, Jamaica. Stronghold of the buccaneers under the great and terrible Henry Morgan, trading centre of the island, chief mart and clearing house for the slave trade, Port Royal by the end of the seventeenth century had become the richest and wickedest city in the world.

With a population of some 8,000, with its vast warehouses and sumptuous cut-stone homes as dear-rented as if they stood in the streets of London, the wicked port was at the very height of its fame and fortune by the year 1692 when, without warning, came disaster and destruction, utter and complete! On June the 7th of that year one of the worst earthquakes in recorded history shook the town to its foundations and plunged the better part beneath the sea for ever.

The casualties were high and great the variety of deaths the townsfolk suffered. Hundreds were crushed beneath tons of falling masonry and stone as houses collapsed like a pack of cards. Hundreds were drowned, while many, trapped beneath falling walls and beams, suffocated to death or faced a slow and frightful end from starvation or loss of blood. Others fell to destruction from the upper stories of buildings and from towers, while still others were swallowed by the great fissures that opened in the earth then squeezed to pulp when another tremor closed the gaping holes like giant pincer-jaws. A few, more luckless than the rest perhaps, were only partially swallowed when the earth shut up again leaving them in dismal torture with heads and shoulders still above ground, in which appalling state they languished while the dogs of the town came and ate the flesh from off their heads and faces, even before death had set them free.

Death, death on all sides. Death in all shapes and forms. And yet amidst this terrible carnage an extraordinary, almost miraculous thing occurred. A man was swallowed by one of the great shocks which tore the earth and by another spewed forth again alive, a man who was to live for many years to come to tell his remarkable story, the strange and moving story of Lewis Galdy of Port Royal, the man who was buried twice.

On the opposite side of Kingston Harbour, across the channel from Port Royal, at a place called Green Bay, Galdy's tomb lay until a few years ago when it was decided to move the tomb and its contents to the churchyard of St. Peter's, Port Royal. It is a brick-built structure with a thick white marble slab resting on top, on which is carved the Galdy arms (a cock between two mullets in chief and a crescent in base), the crest (a plumed esquire's helmet) and the Galdy motto, *Dieu sur tout*, "God above everything." But this is not all: on the thick white marble slab the story is told in deep-carved letters, as clear to-day as they were two centuries ago. Brief and simple is the epitaph:

Here Lyes the Body of LEWIS GALDY Esqr., who departed this life at *Port Royal* the 22d December 1739. Aged 80 years. He was born at *Montpelier* in *France*, but left that Country for his Religion and came to settle in this *Island*, where he was swallowed up in the Great Earthquake in the year 1692 and by the Providence of God was by another Shock thrown into the *Sea*, and miraculously saved by swimming until a boat took him up: He lived many years after in great Reputation, Beloved by all who knew him and much lamented at his death.

Briefly and simply told, and yet it tells so much. Galdy the Huguenot, born in Montpellier the year before the last Spanish Governor of Jamaica fled defeated from the north coast and the island finally fell to the English invasion force. Montpellier, chief town of Languedoc, capital of the department of Hérault, had been a place of importance from as early as the eighth century. Famous for its ancient schools of medicine and law, its thirteenth century university, its celebrated botanic garden, Montpellier was also one of the centres of the Huguenots, French Protestants who first appeared during the sixteenth century. Persecution of these reformers began almost immediately with an edict of 1535 and went on steadily for two hundred years. Among the people who were forced to flee France was John Calvin. Less famous, but perhaps no less sincere, was Lewis Galdy of Montpellier, driven from his country, says his epitaph, because of his religion.

Intelligent and industrious, a man of breeding and ability, charming in manner and attractive in person, Galdy came to settle in the island, at Port Royal, to make a home and a name and a fortune for himself. He had a keen business mind and there was ample opportunity for such a person. He set up as a merchant in a modest way at first, but soon his business started to expand; soon he found his fingers in many profitable pies—merchandise, shipping ventures of one kind or another, produce dealing, the slave trade, politics. He was not alone in the field by any means. Competition was stiff, but opportunity was ample, for this, remember, was the end of the seventeenth century, and the wicked Port was at the height of its fame and fortune. This was, in fact, the year 1692, June of that year, the 7th of June to be exact.

The day dawned dully. This was one of the things that Galdy noticed as he walked down to his office near the waterfront. This, and the fact that the atmosphere was hot and sultry, that the coppery sky glowed like a furnace while the sea, oil-flat and weed-clogged, lay unruffled by a single breath of air. The harbour was filled with shipping, among the vessels being two just back from a successful raid on the French settlements in neighbouring Saint Domingue, their rich cargoes having swelled still further the storehouses and bulging pockets of the smarter residents of the Port.

The Legislative Council had met that morning for the dispatch of business but, as early hours were the rule, had adjourned before noon. Many of the townsfolk were gathered around the dining table; others, like the President of the Council, had already lunched and were relaxing over a glass of wine and a pipe of choice tobacco at one of the many meeting places near the waterfront when disaster overtook the place.

At twenty minutes to twelve exactly a thunderous noise was heard rumbling in the St. Andrew mountains north of Port Royal; then, within the space of two short minutes three earthquake shocks, each one more violent than the first, broke with a terrible roar beneath Port Royal. Lewis Galdy, who was seeing to rather urgent business at the time, dropped the heavy leather-bound ledger he was perusing and dashed out of his office, nor was he a moment too soon. With an awful groan the whole building keeled over and sank to the ground amidst clouds of dust, powdered lime and mortar. The earth still bucked and trembled as he staggered, half-dazed, along the street—a street which he could barely recognise. Wharves and warehouses, residences, taverns and stews, all were disappearing, even as he looked, into the sea as the land tilted crazily like the deck of a sinking ship. Although there was no wind the sea rose in mighty waves, tearing the vessels from their moorings and sweeping them over the sunken ruins of the town; some were utterly destroyed while others rode out the tidal wave, their masts intermingling with the spires of the sunken churches.

Galdy found his wild flight down the street halted when the earth suddenly opened up not ten yards ahead of him and the rest of the street vanished in the abyss. Stumbling back, he next thought of Morgan's Fort as a possible place of safety and dived down a narrow alley which led to it. But there a bewildering sight broke on his view: where the fort had stood was now the open sea! He wheeled once more towards the stricken heart of the town, but before he had taken a dozen steps a great hole opened under his feet and he began to fall down, down into the earth . . .

Afterwards, whenever he told the story, Galdy always paused at that point, for that was the last thing he remembered clearly. Of the other earthquake shock which miraculously threw him forth into the sea, of his frantic swimming round and round, and of his eventual rescue by some people in a boat, he mercifully remembered very little.

Lewis Galdy, like Port Royal itself, was in time to recover from the catastrophe of 1692. Slowly he built up his business again and the great fortune that had vanished beneath the waves that summer day. Politics interested him and he sat, at different times, as member of the House of Assembly not only for Port Royal parish, but for St. Mary, the old parish of St. George (where Portland is to-day), and even for distant

St. Ann. A devout and public-spirited man, Galdy found time despite his many other occupations to identify himself with religious matters, and was one of the two Church-wardens who directed the rebuilding of the Parish Church of St. Peter at Port Royal.

Fourteen years later the end came suddenly, peacefully. They buried him at Green Bay, across the channel from Port Royal, and on the spot they raised a brick-built tomb with a thick white marble slab on top, on which the story is told in deep-carved letters, as clear to-day as they were two centuries ago, the story of the man who was buried twice, the strange and moving story of Lewis Galdy of Port Royal.

The Square, St. Jago de la Vega

The Golden Table

ONE OF THE most persistent of Jamaican legends tells of a great golden table which lies concealed at the bottom of many of our rivers and deep silent ponds. This fabulous table, rich beyond imagining, is said to appear briefly from time to time to tempt frail humans almost to distraction with desire; but it is better never looked upon and best let alone, for it is unattainable and to pursue it is to pursue disaster.

The legend is widespread: there can scarcely be a parish in the island which does not boast a golden table; and it is alive: many people devoutly believe in the table's existence and a few even claim to have seen it. There is a boy in St. Thomas who swears he knows a pond with a golden table and is quite sure that he can show it to me, if only I will go with him. I know an old gardener of St. Andrew who saw his golden table in the Hope River, and how real a vision it had been!—"The legs are as big as *this*," he told me with firm conviction, showing me his massive forearm. I knew a property owner, a person who understood a legend for what it was, who nevertheless declared that she could never take her horse quietly past a certain pond on the property in which —so it was said—a golden table lay.

How did this strange legend come to life, and where? Where? There are many people who are in no doubt whatever on this point. I have stood with some of them on the bank of the Rio Cobre not far from Spanish Town and stared at the very spot in the river where *the* Golden Table is said to be. The neighbouring pen-keepers and the people of the district all know the spot and will point it out for you; so will the small boys who fish for jonga in the muddy waters, and they know the river well:

"What is the name of this place?" You ask them, just to see.

"*Golden Table*," comes the answer. "But don't trouble it."

"Why?"

"You will dead. Anybody trouble it . . . dead!"

"The Rio Cobre," wrote a Dr. Jasper Cargill in 1892, "after leaving its broad bed in old Berry, now Enson Pen, meandered in a tortuous course through the wooded pastures, and just as it emerged from the thick forest of trees into the open space above 'Three Meetings' wound round some rocks, forming a deep sluggish pool, before running swiftly over a cluster of small boulders, which we used to call the 'rapids' above the bathing place at 'Three Meetings.' It was in this pool that the 'Golden Table' was supposed to be."

The writer goes on to say that he was told the Irrigation Works had so altered the course of the Rio Cobre that the bathing places, as well as the pool which contained the "universally believed in and much dreaded 'Golden Table'" were now unrecognisable.

As far as I can discover, the Irrigation Works did not actually alter the course of the river. They changed its character, if you will, by turning away so much of the water into the hot fields of the plain, so that at certain times it is possible to walk long distances up the dry river bed, but it is the same bed, and at such times if you wish you can stand on the very spot where the *table* is supposed to be.

Otherwise the writer is correct. To bring his record up to date: Berry Pen is now called Ensom, the Berry Pen Road is known to-day as the Gordon Pen Road, and "Three Meetings" has shrunken to "Two." For the rest, there are the same wooded pastures and trees; the strange rocks and small boulders; the same wide "open space" where the Cobre makes its turn, called "Broad Water"; and, when the river is in spate, the deep sluggish pool where the Golden Table is said to lie concealed.

Here it was (so goes the story), long ago, before the changes, if one were bold enough to stand on the river's edge and look down into the deep pool, dead on the stroke of noon, he would see the Golden Table rise in shimmering glory from the water and hang motionless on the surface for twelve short seconds. He would see the sunlight pouring through the wide-spread arms of the old guango trees, draw strange fire-like flashes from its wide top, then, rapidly, it would sink from sight, sucking down with it whatever chanced to float close by at the time, and what sank with the Golden Table never rose again. So, at least, went the story.

"Once from the deck of a man-of-war," continues Dr. Cargill, "I saw a large shark slowly rise from the sea and take into its dreadful jaws a guard fish that had just been shot by an officer with his rifle, and then sink leisurely back into its deep home, leaving some bubbles to mark the spot for a few moments; such in my imagination was the rising and sinking of the 'Golden Table.' Scientific sceptics affirmed that it was an optical illusion, and explained the matter thus:— The sun at noon being over-head, and its rays, shining through the opening in the trees, played on the *copper* bottom of the river, causing for a few seconds the appearance of a gold-coloured surface, but," adds the writer, "this was never verified by these scientists diving to the bottom of the blue hole with hammer and chisel and chipping off a piece of the supposed copper."

So bathers shunned the place, preferring the pool at "Three Meetings." But this was long ago, before the changes, before the water was turned into the hot fields of the plain, before it was possible to walk long distances up the dry river bed and stand, if you wished, on the very spot where the Table is said to be, a spot that men still shun. "Don't trouble *it*," they advise: "anybody trouble it . . . dead!"

And yet through the years, before the changes, many must have watched the Table rising dead on the stroke of noon, as the sunlight poured through the widespread arms of the old guango trees. Many must have seen and many coveted the rich metal and the good things that it could buy for its owner. There must have been many such, but the story of only one survives, the story of the St. Catherine planter who tried to take the evil Table from the Rio Cobre.

We know little about the man. Legend here is miserly with its details. We do not know his name nor the name of his plantation. Somewhere on the hot plains he had his canefields and his sugar-works. Some day, some ill-fated day he must have heard the story of the Golden Table, a strange story which caught his interest and imagination. The journey from his plantation was an easy one on horseback and he started in good time. Down to St. Jago de la Vega he rode, keeping well away from the Parade and busy sections of the town with their threat of delay through chance encounters, then out on the Berry Pen Road white and dusty under a blazing sun, to the place where the narrow bridle track struck out across a field grown thick with divi divi and savage thornbush, down the winding path past soursop trees and small-leaved ebonies covered with yellow blooms, to the appointed spot on the steaming river bank.

The sweat gathered on his forehead then rolled in streams down his face as he waited, tense, silent, that first time, beside the giant ceiba cotton tree, its massive limbs thick with flowering parasites and the thin tendrils of long trailing withes

—waited for the apparition of which he had been told, in which he hardly dared believe, till, dead on the stroke of noon, it came.

Twelve seconds went by, then the Table was gone. Twelve brief seconds: a short time, but long enough for the birth of a daring resolve, a rash imprudent plan to wrest the Golden Table from the river.

Within a week all was in readiness. Twelve yoke of oxen were drawn up on the river bank at the appointed place and harnessed to a stout cattle chain at the end of which were fastened grappling irons. Three slaves, stripped naked, crouched at the water's edge ready to dive into the pool and fix these grapnels; a tall young slave boy stood at the head of the monster team holding the lead-ropes while two others bearing long raw-hide cattle whips waited for the signal to urge the steers forward. Twenty-four steers, maddened by the lash, heaving and plunging up the river bank, would surely be sufficient to pull even the Golden Table from the water?

Then it came, dead on the stroke of noon. Through dry, caked lips the planter counted the seconds . . . would the swimmers never reach the Table! . . . go on, go on, fix the grapnels to the legs, only hurry! . . . the lash, you fools, the lash! . . . again, again!

The Table began to sink. To the planter, from his place slightly higher up the river bank beside the giant cotton tree, the group at the water's edge seemed suddenly to have petrified—then the Table vanished, dragging with it the struggling oxen and six screaming slaves. For a time the water eddied swiftly in the deep pool, then slowly settled. From the thick branches of an old frou-frou tree a gaulin flew leisurely up-stream.

Legend here is miserly with its details. We do not know the planter's name nor the name of his plantation. Somewhere on the hot plains he had his canefields and his sugar-works. Somewhere on those same plains to-day on what is now Caymanas Estates property is a field with a strange story.

Beneath the green cane, say the people of the district, a plantation house and its sugar-works lie buried. When or how the disaster came about they do not know, but they believe the story implicitly.

Could this have been the house of the St. Catherine planter who tried to take the Golden Table from the river? Is it too fanciful to think that fate, perhaps in some grim earthquake form, dragged to his doom—as the Table had done his steers and six screaming slaves—the man who had dared too much?

Fate: it is remarkable how prominent is its role in the story. If this is a legend of anything it is the legend of retributive justice. Fate: the very vessel's name was *Nemesis*. Once a trim ship of the line, *Nemesis* was now a hunted outlaw with a price on her head, or rather on the heads of those who sailed her. Large, full-rigged, with black painted hull and no country's colours at the mast-head, she had skulked around the Caribbean with one hawk's-eye on the lookout for prey, the other searching for the warship always on her track. Her port-holes covered by canvas, concealed six carronades on each side, while draped in black cloth at the stern was the long, eighteen-pound swivel gun which had held off many an attack.

So far fortune had been liberal to the mutinous crew of the *Nemesis* since the fateful day they threw the butchered body of their commander and most of his officers into the sea and took over the ship. Since then there had been the usual ups and downs: stiff engagements with armed merchantmen and Naval craft from which *Nemesis* had emerged battered and profitless. The deck had run with blood and some of the original crewmen had long since joined their fellows at the sea bottom; but most of the oldtimers were still there: Burchett the bull-like ex-boatswain, for example, now captain of the freebooters; and lean, red-bearded Jackson, ship's carpenter, an asset to any crew. Jackson the sly and saturnine, handy alike in a fight or round the council table; Jackson who always seemed to know what ships to tackle and when best to strike. And there had been fat prizes and rich takings, slow, wallowing galleons, freighted deep with plate and coin from the Main, destined for the coffers of His Most Catholic Majesty. There had been these, and smaller game too, with less profitable cargoes, but easier and safer to take. Yes, on the whole fortune had been liberal to the mutinous crew of the *Nemesis,* and now with their rich loot stowed safely below decks they did what few pirate crews ever managed to do, take time out to think about the future.

Burchett it was who eventually put the result of their deliberations into words. Jackson stood at his side when he spoke and the hard-bitten crew felt more at ease for they were better at fighting than thinking and trusted the counsel of their carpenter more even than they did their captain's. Roughly the idea went like this.

Fortune had been pretty decent, all things considered. Shared according to the usual rules there was enough yellow gold in the brass-bound chests stowed below to make every man on board secure for life, that is if he didn't blow it all in the Port Royal taverns or waste it on the whores. But Fortune herself was a whore, fickle and inconstant. Perhaps they shouldn't try her favours further. Times were changing. This was October of the year 1662: it was already two months since Lord Windsor had arrived in Jamaica as governor. They had had it on good authority that one of his particular instructions was to settle judicatories for Council affairs and for the Admiralty. Already the blustery trade winds were carrying aloft the groan of gibbet chains on sinister Gallows Point. Matters were looking less and less favourable for the filibuster, especially those of the *Nemesis* against whose names the Admiralty had set a particular mark in their black books. Why not pull out now, while the pulling was good?—land the loot in Jamaica, sink the ship and each man with his own share of coin go his way, settle down in the island or move on to another, mix with the colonists and start a new life. A change of name and a tight lip and all would be well.

The reasoning was sound and seemed to find general approval. All that remained was to implement the plan.

On a pitch black stormy night, shortly after the meeting, the *Nemesis* appeared off Great Pedro Bluff on Jamaica's south coast, tacking slowly closer in, finally dropping anchor in a small deserted bay. The darkness and foul weather suited the filibusters admirably for they removed the risk of detection, but the wind and driving rain made the work harder and more hazardous. Laboriously the chests of gold were transported from ship to shore and concealed in a place called "Jack's Hole" near the Pedro Plains.

Eventually that was done and all that remained was to send the *Nemesis* to the bottom, then *Hurrah!* for a life of ease and plenty ashore—decent citizens of this new colony of Jamaica, loyal subjects of His Majesty King Charles, men of substance and worth, gentlemen even, with large plantations, rich food, good drink and the velvet-soft arms of black slave girls to comfort and delight.

These were the pictures that filled the minds of the pirate crew that stormy October night. In spite of the cold, wet weather they went about the business in high spirits. It was such a good plan, they all felt—all, that is, except the ship's carpenter, Jackson, the sly and saturnine. For a long time he had been thinking about the future, but along rather different lines from the others and as he helped with the transporting of the stout mahogany chests he had thought out a better plan, a very different plan from that which Burchett had proposed.

He had no faith in these pretty pictures of reformed pirates living decent, prosperous lives on land. There were twenty-nine men aboard the *Nemesis* beside himself. Twenty-nine to share the loot. They would get a fair share each, but not enough to buy plantations, madeira and black mistresses, not unless each man worked like hell, and that was the one thing Jackson knew they would not do. Life ashore was a different matter from life at sea. In a new colony like Jamaica a man must struggle to establish himself and his holdings. He must reckon with crop failure, hurricane, flood, drought, the possibility of invasion and local revolts and strife. At sea it was easy come, easy go. The only virtue a man needed was courage, the only equipment his cutlass and firearms. The prospects were simple: success or failure, gold or the gallows, or if you were lucky a bullet in the guts and death anyway was at the end of it all, sooner or later.

But life ashore was a different matter. These men were a drunken, stupid, cut-throat lot. They would never really work, Jackson was sure of that; they would blow their swag in the stews and they would blab; once in their liquor they would talk about the *Nemesis* and their shipmates: a chance remark perhaps, little more than a name or date, but who knew where it would end? A Navy man might hear the name. It would be enough. They had ways of making even pirates talk.

Then what of the rest of the crew, what of himself? Hunted as the runaway slaves were hunted, shot down like a beast or hung in chains on some sun-baked cay off the Palisadoes. No, he had not risked his neck these last twelve months to have it stretched because some drunken bastard had talked too much. Besides, the booty was not all *that* large. To one man it could spell ease and comfort indeed, acres of sugar cane, good living, succulent wenches; but shared among thirty the treasure shrank to mean and futile proportions. Furthermore, how did he know that it would be shared after all? How could he tell what was in the mind of Burchett for instance, or of any of the others? Why should he run the risk of being cheated now or betrayed later? Why indeed, when it was so easy not to, so easy to have it all to oneself—safe and rich, decent citizen, loyal subject, man of substance, a title perhaps! Great plantations, wine, soft arms . . . rich and safe. And it could be done. He, Jackson, could do it.

Yes, send the *Nemesis* to the bottom, he agreed, but first a good carouse with the last of the rum and a toast or two to the good ship and to the future, whatever that might hold!

The future held very little for Jackson's twenty-nine shipmates. He managed to dope the cask of rum, making sure to drink none of the stuff himself. Within an hour the crew of the *Nemesis* were sprawled insensible about the deck. Hurrying below Jackson fixed a slow match to the powder magazine then scrambling back to the deck he climbed down to the waiting dinghy and rowed hard for the shore. He had barely struggled through the rough surf of the rain-lashed beach when there was a sudden burst of light and flame and a deafening explosion as the *Nemesis* half lifted from the flame-coloured waters like a rearing horse, then started on the long slow dive to the seabed.

But can one really rid oneself of nemesis? Jackson thought so, Jackson the sly and saturnine, standing on the rain-soaked sands of the little, deserted bay on that stormy October night of the year 1662, standing and smiling grimly as the ship sank to the bottom of the sea taking with her his twenty-nine shipmates—twenty-nine mouths shut for all time, twenty-nine pairs of hands that would never reach scarred, black-nailed fingers to clutch at the gold that was now his, all his!

He knew of course that he must proceed with caution, great caution, if the rest of his scheme were to succeed. Taking only enough money to keep him from starvation for a short time, he set out to look for work on the plantations. Here there was no difficulty at all, carpenters were much in demand in the new colony and there was ample work to do wherever he went. Besides, he was a competent fiddler and knew many catchy songs which he played well; so when he grew tired of hammer and saw he would shoulder his fiddle and push on, playing wherever and whenever his services were needed, at parties or weddings, in tavern or great house.

In this way the ex-pirate drifted from town to town earning a fair wage and spending as little as he could, listening a good deal but not saying much, mixing with all kinds of people and skilfully building a reputation for respectability and thrift—the first step towards his kingdom—and on the lookout for the right place in which to settle down, a place where a man could live with little interference from prying neighbours and acquaintances, a place where there was the chance to make a fortune—or appear to do so, and a place where a man might spend that fortune on the things that made wealth worthwhile.

In St. Jago de la Vega, the old Spanish capital on the banks of the Rio Cobre, and still the chief town of the island, Jackson found such a place. It was suited to his purpose in every way. One of the new Governor's particular instructions was to direct the repair of the houses in the city, so Jackson the carpenter found his services in immediate demand. He worked at first on restorations to the buildings despoiled by the invading army, then later on repairs to the Spanish Chapel of the Red Cross, badly damaged by the zealous Cromwellian troops but now rededicated to their own faith. From these occupations Jackson began to turn his attention increasingly to furniture making, a more skilled and better paid business. Soon he opened a small shop in the town where for a time he took in work from the neighbouring planters and wealthy residents of St. Jago, gradually refusing orders on the pretext of being too occupied to fill them all, as indeed he was but not with his craft. He was busy searching for the ideal site for the house he intended to build, the house in which he could store in safety the vast fortune in rich gold buried in Jack's Hole near the Pedro Plains, buried like the *Nemesis* and her crew of twenty-nine, but not so deep or irrecoverably.

But can one really bury nemesis? Nemesis? Jackson thought so—Jackson the popular, prosperous furniture maker of St. Jago, standing in his shop one evening in late August, standing and thinking that now the time had come for the next move in his daring scheme, the next huge step towards his kingdom.

First he bought the land: four acres on the Berry Pen Road, suitably remote from city and neighbours, with the wide Rio Cobre itself for one boundary. The next task was to build the house, a small, unpretentious house, the erection of which he himself could assist and supervise. In fact, he needed little help with the job except for a couple of apprentices and three or four Negro slaves whose services he dispensed with even before the house was complete ostensibly in the interests of economy. But the real reason was the need for privacy as he worked on the cellar beneath the main bedroom destined to be the secret hiding place of his great fortune.

Safe from prying eyes Jackson laboured stealthily and tirelessly on the deep and sturdy vault with its flight of cut-stone steps, elaborate spring-lock, and trap-door of solid hardwood which fitted when closed so nicely with the rest of the flooring as to be unnoticeable.

And finally, the transportation of the treasure all the way from the Pedro Plains to St. Jago, a formidable task; one that required infinite care and cunning, patience and time. Yes, it took time and it required patience, but it was done at length, and Jackson knew complete content the night he packed the last brass-bound chest in its corner, mounted the flight of cut-stone steps and let the heavy trap-door of the vault fall back into place with a safe and final thud.

It would be difficult to describe the deep content that possessed him, the intoxicating sense of fulfilment at a daring and dangerous task well accomplished. Surely he had earned the treasure and all that it could mean to its owner. How wrong, how unspeakably wrong and unjust it would have been to share such wealth with a crew of stupid, half-drunken brutes when *he* had the brain, the daring and ability to keep it all himself. The swag was his. By God he had earned it. Rot them! they would never reach their scarred and black-nailed fingers to clutch at his gold now safe in his secret cellar. They were gone to hell, they and the *Nemesis*. Neither they nor anyone else would lay hands on Jackson's treasure. He had worked and schemed too much to lose it now. He had dared too much and longed too hard to let it out of his clutches . . .

The *sweet trade*, they called it, the deck running with blood, the air thick with smoke and powder, the curses and the shouted orders, the screams of pain and the choking rattle in the throats of dying men. And then the booty: jewels and rich stuffs, velvet, silk and gold cloth, gold and silver plate, and coins, coins smooth and round and grateful to the touch, warm and winking in the bright sunlight, the warmth soothing the sting of stab wound, the agony of broken bone, making all well again, making all worthwhile, making all things righteous, even the blood and the slashed throats, the torture and the rape, even the betrayal of one's shipmates —the slow match at the powder magazine, the flash and roar, then the long dive to the bottom of the sea, the long, slow dive to hell! Making all well again, making all worthwhile— a man of standing and substance (with the past forgotten, wiped out) broad acres of sugar cane, good food and drink and the velvet-soft arms of many women to comfort and delight.

What could a man not do with so much wealth! The possibilities were limitless, the vista which they opened stretched far out of sight. He needed time to plan the future carefully. He must proceed with caution. No use hurrying. Fatal to make a false step. Not likely. Not Jackson. He was too clever for that. He had worked too hard and risked too much to spoil things now . . .

How agonising had been that time, those years, when the treasure had lain buried on the Pedro Plains. How great the anguish of this separation from his gold. He had not fully realised the depth of his suffering then, but now, now that they were re-united, like a man with his wife, now he understood, by contrast, how great must have been the pain of separation.

Well, that was all past. Never again would they be parted, he and his gold. No one, nothing could come between them now.

The hours had stretched into days, then weeks, before Jackson seemed so much as to remember his furniture business up in the city. The idea seemed suddenly remote and unreal to him. One day he locked up the house carefully and walked into the town, to his shop. Hanging from a rusty bracket was a mean and faded sign proclaiming his name and occupation. He stared stupidly at it, saying over and over to himself, "That's you, you . . ."

But was that really so? That *was* he. That was now part of the past, a remote and unreal past. Everything was changed now. He had no part in this strange person whose name was on the sign. No part, it seemed, in anything he saw—the market with its noisy, colourful crowd, the street-side stalls and booths with vendors calling the merits of their cheap wares, the churches with their pointed steeples, the shops and warehouses, the inns and taverns, the cool, tile-roofed residences of the townfolk. No part in the life of these people —the seaman with his ear-rings and red bandanna, leaning against the wall of the rum-shop, the comely serving wenches, the soldiers in their bright tunics, the planters from the neighbouring estates, the workmen and the slaves, the beggar at the street corner, the starving dog that lapped the milky water from the stinking gutter.

Who were these people who seemed to know his name and called after him as he turned with scarce a nod of recognition and started back down the side street towards his house on the Berry Pen Road, started back without so much as opening the door of his shop, back to his treasure, to his world, to life, the real life, not this make-believe shadowy world of St. Jago. Already he had been away from his treasure too long. Suppose anything should happen in his absence. Suppose someone were to break in. It was madness to leave his house, his world, so long. Madness.

Madness. *Madness*, people began to whisper: how else could they account for Jackson's strange behaviour? Why had he stopped working? Why did he pretend not to know his friends? Why had he secluded himself in his little house on the Berry Pen Road, seldom stirring from it except to work in his vegetable garden?

Madness, surely—this complete neglect of himself and his appearance. The unkempt hair and beard, the ragged clothes, the starved emaciated look. Or was there something else the matter? Was he really in need? If so why had he given up his work? There was good money to be made these days in the furniture business, and he had done well. Yet why did he accept the alms of strangers who, meeting him on the rare occasions that he ventured out, were often moved to pity by the haggard, destitute figure he presented?

Why, indeed? He was always a strange one. Come to think of it nobody really knew much about him. During his early years in the city he had managed to say very little about himself, and now that he mixed and spoke with no one it was impossible to discover more.

Madness? Perhaps. For a time people whispered and wondered, then they forgot. Jackson was harmless enough, uninteresting enough. Soon the change in the man was scarcely noticed and he took his place, such as it was, among the dull, lesser-known and half-forgotten features of the town. There was too much that was new and interesting happening in the island for Jackson to claim attention long. More than a dozen administrators of varying type and calibre had regulated the affairs of the country since he had settled in St. Jago and all had left their mark on the changing picture of the new colony and of the Caribbean itself, few perhaps more clearly than had the buccaneer-governor Sir Henry Morgan. Morgan whose relentless private war with Spain had served a hard-pressed Britain well and helped to keep Jamaica safe; Morgan the victor of Puerto Príncipe, Porto Bello, Maracaibo; Morgan the incredible Welshman who had led a rabble army against rich and glittering Panama itself—the very heart of Spain's great might in the New World—and burnt it to the ground! Morgan and his exploits were on everybody's lips, all Jamaica resounded to his fame, but behind the closed doors of the little house on the Berry Pen Road not the faintest echo penetrated, or if it did it left the ex-pirate of St. Jago quite unmoved, his blood unstirred by the doings of the greatest pirate of them all.

Now even Morgan was dead. At last he had coughed the demon tuberculosis out of his lungs and was dead, drinking, they said, and cursing, laughing, scheming with his old friend Albemarle, the new governor, to the end. Now Albemarle also was gone, his heart and bowels buried beneath the altar of the town's chief church which Jackson himself had helped to restore, his body soaked in pitch and sealed in many coffins sent back to England for interment. But behind the closed doors of the little house on the Berry Pen Road the news scarcely reached, or if it did it left the ex-carpenter of St. Jago quite unmoved.

Behind those closed doors was a new world all its own, a small, personal world which had no relation to the one outside; a narrow world since it contained one man alone, but to that man it was vast, a whole kingdom. It was not created suddenly or rapidly. It took time. Its evolution was slow. It began to take shape that first day after the treasure had been transported from the Pedro Plains, the day Jackson went up into the city to his shop. It was then that he first realised how make-believe, how unreal had been his life during the separation from his treasure. Everything was different once he was back in his house on the Berry Pen Road. There, suddenly, was security and stability and in the contemplation of the things his gold could buy him the things he already knew and owned seemed suddenly unreal.

Gradually the idea had so possessed him that the abstract dreams of the future became the immediate thing and the real life around him only a symbolisation of events. So, day after day he lived his changing chosen dream-life more keenly than man ever really lived, arranging and altering as he desired, over and over.

At a thought, a wish, the great house he had set his heart upon rose up for him, complete and perfect against its glorious mountain background; the green, shimmering fields of sugar cane waved in the warm breeze and on the portico of his mansion he surveyed his kingdom, a kingdom that stretched far out beyond the confines of the plantation.

Then the scene would change and it is autumn and he moves up to the city for the sessions of Assembly. He dines with the governor and at balls and social gatherings smiles at the scarce-concealed advances and admiration of the many grand ladies who would gladly be his wife. The governor calls him friend and counsellor and, leaning his wigged head close, often seeks his views on weighty matters of state. His voice shapes policy and at his word men are raised up or dashed with their broken hopes. His name is spoken in Whitehall and already there is talk of a title.

Sometimes, however, the pictures would fade and Jackson would see for a moment the drab walls of his narrow room, the mean furnishings, and know for what it was his small life with its short hopes; and he would realise that the visions that went before were dreams, images only of the things his gold could buy him, that he must open the chests to make the visions come true, that he must part with his gold.

Part with his gold!—better part with himself, as indeed he would be doing since he and the gold were now one. How much must he spend? Where would the spending end? Plantations cost money, so did fine houses and fine clothes. The governor valued his counsel but needed ready cash as well. Everything had its price—the dinners and balls, the social gatherings and grand ladies with their soft eyes and arms . . . arms, hands, everywhere he looked he saw hands, hands held out to him, the jewelled fingers of the governor and Whitehall officials, the delicate pink-tipped hands of the women. Gone were the broken, black-nailed fingers of his shipmates, but in their place the hands that now reached towards his treasure were more elegant but equally rapacious.

At such times Jackson would press his own hands over his eyes to shut out the awful picture, forcing his mind back to the kind images and dreams, back to the world that was his for the asking. Soon the drab walls would fade and once more the great house on which he had set his heart would rise up for him, complete and perfect, and on the portico he could stand and survey his kingdom—happy again and contented, but lost beyond all hope of recovery, sunk deep like the ship and her crew of twenty-nine, dragged to the bottom and drowned in the blood-stained treasure of the *Nemesis*.

Day after day Jackson lived in his golden world, toying with his treasure and his dreams, plunging his hands deep down into the chests of rich metal, letting the coins flow in streams through his fingers as he picked up handful after handful of the precious stuff—golden days which spun slowly into weeks and months, into years.

One day, without warning, he must have grown tired of the game, or impatient at its limitations, or perhaps suddenly very fearful of the voice which still whispered inside him at odd times, though now less frequently, that the only way to possess his treasure was to spend it. Whatever the reason he began to cast about for a better, safer way of enjoying his gold and at the same time of securing it more surely. He did not have to ponder the problem long. Soon he had the solution, and once more he was content. Besides, it gave him something new to do, something that needed energy and thought and the half-forgotten skill of the carpenter.

He chose the wood with great care, for it must last a long time, in fact it must last for ever. Although he worked long and hard at the job it took him more than a month to complete. But what was that to Jackson now? It was time well spent, for the table, strongly and beautifully made, was worthy to receive his rich and noble treasure.

The next task was to remove the chests from the cellar and lift down the table in their place. This too took time and effort. But what was that to Jackson now? He had all the time in the world and the effort was such loving labour. It was the same with the coins: he took his own sweet time nailing them down with small brass tacks on the table top. He did not hurry the work, he lingered over it, relishing to the full each rich and regal moment as he nailed the golden discs in quaint designs and patterns only to torture them into other shapes and figures by adding lines and other varied geometric forms. Soon the top then the sides and legs of the table were completely encrusted. Still he nailed down the coins— beneath the table top, under the feet—till there was not a trace left of the mahogany below, till not a single gold-piece remained in the sturdy, brass-bound chests.

Now at last was his joy really complete; now all he had to do was reach out his arms to possess his treasure entirely; now everything was his at one grasp, with the danger of spending a single golden coin to obtain it removed for ever. How poor had been his early dreams—respectability, plantations, food, drink and women for his delight and comfort. How paltry, shabby, mean and humble were these compared with the enjoyment of his great Golden Table. There had never been such a one before and there never would be. The greatest princes and potentates, kings and emperors of all time had dreamed of such a possession, but had never known it! This was food and drink, honey and manna from heaven; this was position, sublime and godlike; and untold joy such as no woman could provide. This was the supreme moment . . . and just as well, because it was the last.

It had been raining for a long time before Jackson seemed to become aware of it. It had in fact been raining for days, for this was the wet season, this was October of the year 1691— twenty-nine years to the very month since that other stormy October night when the *Nemesis* sank off Great Pedro Bluff with twenty-nine souls on board. Twenty-nine! Was there some fatal significance in the number? It is doubtful that Jackson was struck by this or wondered much about the possibility. He had passed wondering about most things now. Indeed, it was only because the rain had gone on for so long that he had noticed it at all. The continuous lightning and thunder had slowly broken in upon his consciousness, as well as another sound, the sound of a great and distant roar that seemed to be coming closer and closer.

Morning had broken when he moved uncertainly to a window and looked out. It was still raining heavily and, to his growing horror, he realised that the Rio Cobre had overflowed its banks. Already his land was flooded to a depth of some two feet while the distant roar of the rising flood grew steadily louder. Amidst the confused and deafening noises Jackson thought at times he could hear the sound of voices crying for help, or sometimes calling his name. The chances are that no one heard his own despairing cries and certainly there were no witnesses to his last moments of panic and dismay as the swirling, coppery water rose relentlessly to sweep the house and its mad inmate to destruction.

Just before the collapse, Jackson struggled down the steps of his cellar for the last time. He was there when the walls gave and the water, freed by the removal of the barrier, seemed to leap into the air then plunged down into the vault. He was there, clutching the table, clinging to his golden world to the end.

The rain had stopped by then and on the river bank a group of people had gathered in an anxious, chattering knot, speculating on Jackson's chances of survival. It was nearly midday and the rain had stopped. Overhead the clouds raced wildly westward, thin, fleecy clouds which parted for a brief moment just as the little house collapsed and a cry went up from the people on the river bank, parted and let a single beam of sunlight through which, swore the onlookers, fell for a few seconds only (no more than twelve, they afterwards declared) upon the glorious, gleaming top of a golden table which, even as they stared, vanished as the roaring waters of the Rio Cobre filled the cellar and rose higher and higher above the wide new course the raging river had carved for itself.

General Robert Venables

The Mission that Failed

ON THE 10th of May 1655, an expedition under the command of Admiral Sir Willian Penn and General Robert Venables having failed disastrously in a descent on the island of Hispaniola (the Haiti of to-day) sailed into what we now call Kingston Harbour and captured Jamaica without the loss of a man, although the eventual conquest was to prove more costly and protracted.

This failure at Hispaniola—"the darkest blot on the history

of the Protectorate"—was a blow to Oliver Cromwell which even the taking of Jamaica could not assuage. The real reason for the defeat always remained something of an enigma to him, although many contributing causes (for some of which he was himself to blame) were recognised.

It was known, for instance, that there was jealousy between the military and naval commands: in the words of Venables, Passion usurped the seat of Reason. There was disaffection: both commanders were disloyal to Cromwell as they were to each other and later landed in the Tower of London to answer charges of treason. Instead of trained troops, the Protector sent "Hectors and Knights of the blade, with common Cheats, Theeves, Cut-purses, and such like lewd persons who had long time lived by the slight of hand and dexterity of wit, and were now making a fair progresse unto Newgate, from whence they were to proceed towards Tiborn." There was cowardice in all ranks: Adjutant-General Jackson's sword was broken over his head for his craven conduct, and many of the fugitives were hanged. There was bad leadership, bad organisation, disunion, fear—all of which Cromwell was aware of, yet the failure, and more particularly the conduct of General Venables, remained a mystery to him: perhaps because there was one side of the story he never knew—the role played in the grim drama by a beautiful young Hispaniolan girl who we may call the Doña Maria, for history leaves no record of her name.

It is Christmas Day of the year 1654 as the curtain goes up on the first act of this short, tragic play, and a strong expeditionary force under the joint command of a certain Admiral Penn and General Venables sails from Portsmouth under sealed orders for the West Indies.

On the deck of the flag-ship Venables stands watching the fog-bound coast of England fade slowly in the distance, his thoughts dark and angry as the winter sky. In his inmost heart he knows that the crafty Oliver Cromwell has beaten him at his own game and the knowledge rankles deep.

Cromwell has long regarded him as a potential rival to be closely watched. He, Venables, had rendered eminent services to the Parliament in the relief of Dublin, and in all the principal actions fought in England. He was popular with the army, a rival in military glory with the Usurper himself. His speedy removal from the scene had become imperative for the Protector's peace of mind.

The projected expedition to the West Indies furnished the perfect opportunity, and Cromwell had promptly offered him the military command. Venables had fathomed the motive behind the offer, but accepted nevertheless, for he had a private purpose to serve. He had determined to hoist Cromwell with his own petard by using the forces placed under him in the service of his monarch whose cause he now secretly espoused.

But here again the shrewd Cromwell had won. He had divided the military command between the General, the Admiral and a Council of Commissioners who were invested with the power of controlling all military operations. Instead of the picked troops Venables had hoped he would have been permitted to select, Cromwell had given him an army composed mostly of ruffians, ex-convicts and the outcasts from various regiments; and, as a finishing touch, had shrouded the expedition's departure in uncertainty and mystery by delaying it for months, finally ordering it to sea so suddenly that the supply ships had to be left behind.

Yes, Cromwell had won, and now here he, Venables, was, committed to this venture of which he knew and cared little, but powerless to change the current of events. Small wonder that his thoughts are dark and angry as he stands on the flagship's deck staring at the receding English coastline which, even as he stares, vanishes in the world of night.

Dimly, confused, the sounds of activity on board the ship drift up to the deck, but he scarcely hears them; his mind is far away as he stands, clutching the rail, a tall gaunt figure with white drawn face and eyes like balls of fire glaring into the darkness.

His abstraction is broken at length by a light touch on his arm. He turns impatiently to find his wife, Elizabeth, standing beside him. Slowly his manner changes. The harsh lines fade from his face, the tenseness goes out of him. He takes her in his arms and kisses her hair tenderly.

Yes, Cromwell had won, but not completely, for here at least, he, Venables, had triumphed, and Elizabeth had sailed with him, after all. Her presence on the expedition had already given, and would continue to give, much cause for criticism, but that mattered little. His bride of but a few months, he was determined that she would not be left behind. He had given out that he was minded to settle in the West Indies, so it was necessary for his wife to accompany him: a slender argument at best, since he was under sealed orders and the actual destination of the fleet was unknown. Still it had served his purpose and Elizabeth had sailed with him, after all.

Smoothly the ship rides the steady ground swell, crushing the dark waters into creamy foam in her hurrying wake. Somewhere in the black distance are the other ships of the fleet, stretching away to westward. Somewhere, also, another vessel steers a similar course, a vessel out of Cadiz with a beautiful young girl on board, a girl fresh from a convent in Spain on her way home to Hispaniola, the girl we have called the Doña Maria, since history leaves no record of her name.

Many days pass before the English fleet sights the Spanish vessel. She is chased and soon overhauled. The engagement is brief, the ship boarded, captured and her complement made prisoner.

Venables is watching the operation from his vessel's deck when he sees Maria for the first time. Her presence is a pleasant surprise to him and immediately gives a different colour to the incident. She is described as having a certain "ripeness of womanhood" in addition to her youthful beauty of form and feature—attractions, in short, "that would win the heart of a dotard."

Venables is no dotard at that. Twice married and with a

string of indiscreet liaisons to his credit, he had already acquired a doubtful fame for imprudent subservience to female charms. Wide and varied as his experience has been, however, he has to admit that there is something desirable about this Spanish girl which stirs cravings in him such as he had never felt before, and as he watches her enter the British ship followed by her fussing duenna, he knows he will have no peace until his desires are satisfied.

As the second act opens, we find Maria comfortably installed aboard the warship. Except for the fact that she is in enemy hands and that her future is now uncertain, she has little of which to complain. Her English captors have treated her most chivalrously. Her valuables and other personal possessions have been restored intact; she has been given the freedom of the ship, the use of a private cabin and allowed to retain the services of her duenna.

Venables it is who has been largely instrumental in securing her these concessions. In support of his action he has urged the considerations of her good birth and high connections both in Spain and Hispaniola—connections which, he claims, might be of great value to the expedition later on.

Maria, on her part, while accepting these privileges has relinquished nothing of her dignity and native pride. She is reserved, aloof, latently hostile: and this is a sore disappointment to the General who sees in this attitude the only serious barrier to his desires. In addition, to conceal his designs from his wife and fellow officers, he must press his suit in secret. This Maria suspects and uses the knowledge to best advantage, while meeting his every advance with unmasked disdain.

Slowly, uneventfully, the days lengthen into weeks, until it is now the end of January, 1655, and the expedition has arrived at Barbados. Here, according to instructions, the sealed parchment documents are opened and the destination of the fleet disclosed. The prime objective is the capture of Hispaniola, Spain's prized West Indian possession . . . and the home of the Doña Maria.

Venables receives this intelligence with mixed feelings. Apart from its military significance, he seems to see in it the means of furthering his designs on the Spanish girl. The question was, what exactly would the information mean to her? How would she react to the news that the great armada was destined against her home island, that the military command rested on the man whose attentions she had spurned? What game would she play now? Was her attitude likely to change? Would she view him in a different light, soften towards him perhaps? It was possible. He generally had his way with women in the long run, and this had been a long run, but perhaps the wait would prove worthwhile in the end. Much time and opportunity had been wasted by her stubbornness, but there was no use repining. There was still time left.

That night he finds Maria taking the air on deck. Her manner is as distant as ever and all attempts at conversation end in fruitless silences. She soon finds an excuse for terminating the meeting and retreating towards her cabin. It is then that Venables mentions the subject of the expedition. His words have an immediate effect. She is suddenly disposed to listen to his news. He expected this and now makes the most of it. Casually he explains that the sealed orders were opened that morning and that the destination of the fleet disclosed as Hispaniola!

She starts involuntarily at the news but remains silent, attentive. In the half-light of the deck she seems more beautiful and desirable than ever and it is with an effort that Venables masters the urge to break down all barriers and take her in his arms then and there. An awkward silence succeeds his last remarks, broken at length by Maria who thanks him for his kindness before she retires to her cabin.

Venables takes one step towards the door, but checks himself and walks away, slowly, down the deck. His words have had their effect. For the first time she has been civil to him, almost friendly. Soon he will have his answer. He must wait.

Inside her cabin Maria leans against the door clutching the handle for support, and listens to the retreating footfalls on the deck. The blood has drained from her face, but her hand on the door is firm and steady; she feels sick and empty inside but in the set of her features there is a strange almost sinister resolve.

The curtain goes up on the last act and we find that many changes have taken place since the arrival at Barbados, especially among the leaders of the expedition. Now that the cloud of secrecy surrounding the destination has lifted the need for pretence no longer seems to exist, and one by one the mask each man has worn throughout the voyage is laid aside as useless.

The veiled mistrust with which Penn and Venables have regarded each other now flares into open hostility. Penn has experience as a seaman, but is punctilious in regard to his quality as Admiral, while Venables on his part is unquiet about his military responsibility in its relation with the naval command.

There are many matters of the first importance to be dispatched at Barbados: there is the recruiting of additional men for the army, the arranging for supplies and the drawing up of a broad plan of action, but in the prevailing atmosphere of mistrust and opposition, little can be accomplished.

With the general abandoning of pretences, Venables no longer seems to find it necessary to conceal his infatuation for Maria, who, on her part, seems to resent his attentions less and less. Since that first night at Barbados their meetings have become more frequent and intimate as time has gone on, and with the increasing intimacy the General's ardour has grown. He does not question this change in her. He accepts it as a matter of course. He generally has his way with women, in the end. It is inevitable.

To Maria he turns more and more for the affection and help which he can find nowhere else. Only in her company does the burden of responsibility and care with which he must struggle daily seem bearable. Only because of her is the whole effort worthwhile. Her companionship is the respite he needs most, her love his dearest wish. He can trust no one, depend on no one but her.

Even in the shaping of his military plans he seeks her advice. His intention was to enter the Ozama and take the city in a bold, frontal assault, relying on the element of surprise coupled with superior force of arms to secure the victory. At Maria's insistence, however, he abandons this plan in favour of the more cautious one of running before the wind and landing twelve leagues farther on beyond the Jaina and attacking from the rear. This, she convinces him, is the expedition's only chance of succeeding. The other scheme is foredoomed to failure.

Foredoomed to failure! Sometimes Venables feels that such indeed is the expedition's fate, do what they will. This hazardous venture in which he and his forces will soon be involved seems to cast an ominous shadow before it. The future is confused, insubstantial. He shrinks from it. In Maria he has the present, real, vital, desirable. He grasps eagerly at all this has to offer, all she has to give—love, understanding, counsel . . .

How well Venables followed the advice of the Hispaniolan girl and how nobly it served her people is the climax of the story. Decisively defeated by an enemy who could see the attacking fleet struggling along the coast to windward and so were able to prepare for it, the remnants of the British forces, a third of their number destroyed, staggered back to their ships, set sail and, on the decision of the moment, landed in Jamaica which, as we have seen, they took without much difficulty.

Thus, then, The Mission that Failed. Richard Hill, the distinguished Jamaican naturalist and historian, to whom we are indebted for the account of the part played by the Hispaniolan girl, says he in turn got the story as history from a Don Rafael Rodriques of St. Jago de los Cavalleros, in 1831.

Here too the lady's story ends, except for an epilogue also contributed by Mr. Hill. He tells us that she was restored

The Mission that Failed

to her family in a "quixotic adventure" of General Lambert,
between his exclusion from the act of amnesty at the Restoration, and his reprieve in 1662, when found guilty in the
Court of King's Bench as a regicide—an adventure which
ended the way such adventures often do.

Now that the young lady was safely back with her family,
their one concern was how best to hide the shame and dis-
honour she had suffered at the hands of Venables, and to
consider this her father and brothers met the very night of
her return in grave and solemn conclave.

It was evident to them that the one sure way for the story
to die would be for General Lambert—the man who knew too
much and had too little reason for concealment—to die with
it. But, strong as were their passions, their generous spirits
shrank from the murder of the man who at much personal
risk, in an exploit as daring as it was selfless, an exploit worthy
of the pen of the great Cervantes himself, had brought the
girl safely back to them.

No, there must be another way. In two hours they had
found it. Their faces were set and unsmiling as they entered
the room where Lambert sat comfortably resting from his
recent travels. They were dressed for a journey, clad in high
sea-boots, and coats draped loosely about their shoulders.

Lambert looked up at them. There was little need for
speech. He rose to his feet and slowly collected his accoutrements from off the low, carved table at his side. The gilded
wall-clock struck the hour of midnight as without a word the
small party walked out of the room.

Lambert was later landed from a Cartagena ship belonging
to the family, who were merchants of that city, and marooned
on one of the turtling islands of the Bay of Honduras. But
that was not the end of the story. Luck was with Lambert
and he was picked up soon after by a buccaneer vessel and
made his way eventually to England where he surrendered
himself to justice and went into banishment in the island of
Guernsey.

Anne Bonney and Mary Read

The Women Pirates

IT WAS A CLEAR, sunny November day of the year 1720 that a trim pirate sloop heeling to the fresh land breeze rounded the Point of Negril on Jamaica's west coast and with magnificent impudence dropped anchor in the Bay.

On the vessel's deck Captain Jack Rackham, known up and down the coast as "Calico Jack" the terror of the Caribbean, leaned against the deck rail and viewed the scene before him with a satisfied air. He had reason enough to be satisfied. Battened down below decks was as rich a cargo or Spanish spoil as any Brother of the Coast could desire. The vessel itself was a late contraband prize of the Don, filched by Rackham in the best buccaneer tradition. Even his search for crew replacements had been eminently successful. In the last ten days of October he had scoured every bay and cove on Jamaica's north side, drumming up recruits from the plantations, running at low game the while until he could increase his company sufficiently. At Ocho Rios he had surprised a canoe which had managed, however, to elude his grasp and make port, but at Dry Harbour fortune had been kinder. Here he had found more volunteers than he could use; here, also, he had overhauled a small sloop entering the bay as he was quitting it, relieved her of her cargo, and with admirable unconcern sailed slowly out of port.

Yes, Calico Jack had reason enough to be satisfied. On the whole fortune had been kind. With patience and cunning he had climbed the blood-stained rungs of the ladder of fame until now he had reached the summit and the broad vista spread out before his gaze was fair to see. Of course, his crew had helped him up the ladder considerably. He always smiled when he thought of his crew—a strange, sly smile. Such a crew. Not quite like any other, he always claimed . . . but he never explained what he meant.

No cloud dimmed the vision on that sunny November day. No warning shade from out the future told of the gathering shadows looming even then on the horizon. It was good to be there, good to be alive, good to be Jack Rackham. The occasion called for a celebration.

On shore a small group of people gathered near the water-side, their anxious eyes and gestures turned frequently in the direction of the trim sloop riding the gentle ground swell with a slow graceful roll.

A piragua, a dug-out fishing boat, bobbing up and down on the blue waters of the bay, sailed warily past the pirate. From his place on deck Rackham spied the small craft and lounging to the rails hailed it, bidding the crew come aboard for a pipeful of choice tobacco and a can of flip. The piragua's men hesitated, but not for long. An invitation of that kind did not come their way often, besides it was just possible that the pirate captain would blow their small boat to pieces with one shot from the long gun pointing ominously from the vessel's forepeak out of sheer devilment if his invitation were spurned.

Slowly the fishing boat tacked to larboard, drew up along-side the sloop, and the nine members of her crew clambered up to the deck. It would have been far better for them had they risked the pirate's wrath and ignored his invitation, but fate plays strange tricks, besides their thoughts were fixed on the punch bowl and perhaps on the possibility of joining Rackham's crew, who knows? Certain it is that they did not cast a backward glance towards the horizon where even then the white fleck of a sail was swiftly growing larger against the sky's bright blue.

For weeks that sail had dogged the pirate's path. In his cruise along the north coast Rackham had lingered longer than a man of business ought to have. The canoe which had eluded him at Ocho Rios had carried with it the news of his whereabouts to the Governor, Sir Nicholas Lawes, a man of action and great energy. No sooner did the information reach him than he dispatched a Captain Barnet in a well-armed sloop in quest of the pirate. The Governor's choice was a shrewd one: with dogged patience Barnet had tracked his quarry from cove to cove, always one jump behind, until now at last he was drawing even.

The crew of the piragua had barely seated themselves before the punch bowl when the sloop hove in sight. In a moment the scene was changed aboard the pirate vessel. Finding that the other ship stood directly towards him, Rack-ham hastily weighed anchor and stood off, making a run for it. In answer to his shouted orders all hands, including the men from the piragua, hurried to spread more and more canvas to the wind, and, under the press of so much the sail, the vessel buried her lee rails in the white foam and leapt lightly seaward.

Trim and swift as was the pirate sloop, Barnet's craft having the advantage of the freshening land breeze soon began to outsail her. Relentlessly the hunter bore down on the quarry, the white wave rising to the thrust of her bows and spreading astern in a foamy wake. Using the tactics of the buccaneers Barnet ranged alongside the fleeing craft, from his vessel's deck grappling irons reached for the fugitive, and with drawn

swords and pistols the sailors scrambled over the bulwarks
and on to the deck of the sloop.

The action that followed was bloody but brief. The pirates,
groggy from the effects of the rum punch, lost heart early in
the fight and gave ground before the determined onslaught of
Barnet's men, fleeing to a vain retreat below decks. Two
of their number only held their places, fighting shoulder to
shoulder long after their comrades had retreated, fighting alone
and unaided against the whole of Barnet's crew. Had the
rest of Rackham's men shown half as much courage as these
two members the issue would no doubt have been different.
It is recorded that when the threats of these two fiery pirates
failed to awaken the fuddled spirits of their comrades to a show
of fight, one fired his pistols down the hold, killing a deserter
outright and wounding others.

But even two pirates such as these are no match for a whole
crew and eventually they went down before the sheer weight
of numbers and were captured. The sloop was quickly
brought under control and manned, the conflict ended with
a strange suddenness as fate and the law caught up with Jack
Rackham and his notorious crew on that sunny November day
of the year 1720.

A fortnight later Captain Barnet sailed into Port Royal with
the pirate sloop in close custody to receive the commendation
of his government plus a reward of two hundred pounds, one
hundred for himself and the other to be divided among his
ship's company.

The news of Rackham's capture was enough to shock a
callous world hardened to surprises of the kind, but even that
was to pale into insignificance when at a Court of Admiralty
held at St. Jago de la Vega shortly after, the astonishing
revelation was made that the two fire-eating filibusters who
had staged the sensational last stand on the deck of the pirate
were not men but women disguised as men—Anne Bonney
and Mary Read by name!

The story of these two sea-amazons is a remarkable one.

Tales of Old Jamaica

Captain Charles Johnson, author of *A General History of the Pirates* (first published in 1724), to whom we are indebted for the full account of their lives, was himself acutely aware of the unbelievable nature of their biography.

"The odd incidents of their rambling lives are such," he writes, "that some may be tempted to think the whole story no better than a novel or romance; but it was supported by many thousand witnesses, I mean the people of Jamaica, who were present at their trials and heard the story of their lives upon the first discovery of their sex."

But novel the story is, and romance too of a high order, if true for all that.

In many particulars the lives of Anne and Mary are similar. Circumstances made it necessary for both to shed feminine identity at a tender age and adopt male manners and dress. They were both destined to sail under the Jolly Roger and, what was more remarkable, on the same ship, although it was but a short time before their famous last fight that they became aware of the other's existence and true identity, although for years they had both engaged in similar exploits.

Mary Read was born in England of English parents. Her mother, who married early, had a short and unhappy married life. Soon after the wedding her young seafaring husband left England on a voyage from which he never returned, leaving her with a boy child born some time after his departure.

The widow, who was "young and airy," soon found herself faced with the prospect of having another child and with the difficulty of explaining satisfactorily how she had come by it. She solved her dilemma for a time by leaving London for the country where nobody knew her and where her second child —a girl whom she named Mary—was born.

She remained about four years in the country when, her slender resources exhausted, she found it necessary to return to London. It was then that fate took a hand. Her boy child died suddenly and she hit on the daring stratagem of dressing Mary in the boy's clothes and passing her off as her son.

The Women Pirates

The scheme worked well; even Mary's grandmother was deceived and made her an allowance of a crown a week. Mary was only thirteen when her grandmother died. This meant the end of the allowance, and, with no other means of support, the child was obliged to earn her own living.

Her first job was that of a "footboy" to a French lady, but she quickly sickened of this service and "growing bold and strong and having also a roving mind" she entered herself on board a British man-o'-war. She soon tired of this also and deserted the sea for the army, joining a regiment of foot in Flanders as a cadet, where her courageous behaviour won her the notice and esteem of her officers.

But underneath her soldier's tunic beat a passionate woman's heart which in time she lost completely to a young handsome Fleming, her bedmate and constant companion in arms. Although she managed to conceal her passion she could not hide all the manifestations of that change that takes place in a woman in love. She became forgetful of army routine and negligent in the care of her weapons. These signs might have passed unnoticed but for her new habit of accompanying her companion, unordered, whenever he was dispatched on dangerous missions.

As the days went by her strange behaviour began to be remarked, meanwhile she was finding it increasingly difficult to hide her secret from the soldier himself. At length, says the chronicler, "as they lay in the same tent and were constantly together, she found a way of letting him discover her sex, without appearing that it was done by design."

The Fleming's astonishment quickly gave place to keen delight at the discovery, and he thought of little else but of gratifying his passion with scant ceremony. Mary, however, had other ideas, and he soon found himself courting her for a wife. When the campaign was over she publicly proclaimed her true identity and was married to her former comrade in arms to the unbounded amazement and delight of the regiment, who subscribed liberally towards the couple's housekeeping.

They removed to Breda and there opened an eating-house,

or ordinary, called The Three Horseshoes, where they did a good business, their chief customers being the officers of their old regiment.

As with her mother, Mary's married life was destined to be short. Her husband died suddenly and the Peace of Ryswick being concluded soon after she was forced to close the eating-house for want of custom.

Hedged round with difficulties Mary Read once again donned man's apparel and returned to Holland, where she joined a regiment of foot quartered in one of the frontier villages, forsaking the army later to take passage aboard a Dutch West-Indiaman bound for the Caribbean.

The vessel had the misfortune to fall in with Rackham who seized and plundered her. During the action he was so impressed with Mary's sword-play, costly as it was to himself, that he offered her a berth on his ship (believing her to be a man) which she readily accepted—becoming the second female crew member, though she did not know it at the time: her partner in disguise being none other than Anne Bonney!

Anne, like Mary, was an illegitimate child. Her father was an Irish attorney who lived in a town near Cork, her mother was his housemaid, the liaison which was to result in Anne's birth having taken place while the attorney's wife was spending time in the country for the benefit of her health.

For some time previously the wife had suspected an affair between her husband and the maid, and on her return from the country decided from certain indications that her suspicions were well founded. Her husband had not troubled himself to write to her once during her stay away, and had gone out of town on the very day of her return on some slight pretext. Convinced that his reason for being away was in order to return during the night and spend it with the maid, she cunningly arranged for the latter to sleep elsewhere while she took her place in bed.

"The husband came to bed, and that night played the vigorous lover," writes Captain Johnson. "But one thing

spoiled the diversion on the wife's side, which was the re-
flection that it was not designed for her. However, she was
very passive and bore it like a Christian."

She appears to have been likewise passive over the separation
from her husband that not unnaturally followed. She was
kinder to him than he deserved, for although they continued
to live apart she made him a substantial allowance from her
personal income.

It was some time later that the maid bore the attorney a
daughter which he adopted. They called her Anne. To
conceal its identity he dressed the child as a boy and said that
it was a relative's son. But his wife had her doubts regarding
the child, and discreet investigations revealed that it was not
a boy at all but the maid's daughter. Unwilling to con-
tribute towards its support, she immediately stopped her
husband's allowance.

This was an ugly turn for the attorney who, realising the
futility of further pretence, defied convention and taking the
housemaid home lived openly with her. His conduct soon
became the talk of the town and his practice fell off so sharply
as a result that he was obliged to give up law. He moved to
Cork where he stayed for a time before emigrating to Carolina
taking Anne and her mother with him. Once in America he
soon forsook his legal profession for the more profitable life
of a planter, and in a short time became a prosperous plantation owner and a person of standing in the colony.

In spite of the amenities surrounding her upbringing,
Anne grew into a strapping, boisterous girl whose fierce,
ungovernable temper often got her into trouble. It is said
she once stabbed a servant-maid to death with a clasp-knife
because the latter had dared to censure her conduct!

The sea had a strong attraction for the girl and she fell into
the habit of frequenting the waterfront disguised as a man.
Her father, confident that she would outgrow her wayward
habits, gave her much her own way, setting about meanwhile
to arrange a good match for her; but both his confidence
and his plans were to be rudely smashed one day when Anne

turned up married to a shiftless sailor named John Bonney whom she had picked up in a waterside tavern.

Turned out of doors by her exasperated parent, Anne and her sailor husband knocked about the seafront for a time, eventually making their way to New Providence in the Bahamas—the Sargasso Sea of the world's riff-raff and a notorious pirate rendezvous.

It was about this time that the dashing freebooter Jack Rackham also arrived in New Providence on a strange mission—a mission of repentance. He had come to claim the King's Pardon recently extended to all pirates who swore to eschew their old calling (generally with tongue in cheek) and settle down as quiet, decent citizens.

Rackham had by this time acquired a reputation for himself as a fearless freebooter. In his early years he had served as quartermaster with Vane's company aboard the *Independence*, but he was ambitious and promotion was not long in coming. It happened one day that a French man-o'-war ran across the freebooters between Cuba and Santo Domingo. For reasons of his own Vane declined to engage the Frenchman, much to his crew's disappointment. Rackham disputed Vane's decision, but the latter, says Captain Johnson, "made use of his power to determine this dispute, which in these cases is absolute and uncontrollable, by their own laws, viz. the captain's absolute right of determining in all questions concerning fighting, chasing, or being chased . . . But the next day the captain's conduct was obliged to stand the test of a vote, and a resolution passed against his honour and dignity, which branded him with the name of coward, deposed him from the command, and turned him out of the company with infamy; and with him went all those who did not vote for boarding the French man-o'-war." Rackham was unanimously chosen captain in Vane's stead.

Good fortune smiled on Calico Jack at the start. In his very first cruise as commander he took and plundered a number of vessels, thereby adding to his prestige and personal coffers. But piracy had its ups and downs, and he was in fact rather down on his luck when the publication of the King's Pardon brought with it new hope.

Making his way to New Providence about mid-May of the year 1719, he and some of his old cronies claimed the benefit of the Act of Grace. Selling the spoil he had with him for ready cash, the ex-pirate captain settled down in the island and abandoned himself to a life of ease and debauchery for as long as his money should last.

It was shortly after his arrival that he met Anne Bonney. Anne, who had become the toast of all the waterside taverns, was swept off her feet by the dashing, handsome Calico Jack, whose methods of courting a woman or taking a ship were similar (as one writer puts it)—no time wasted, straight up alongside, every gun brought to play, and the prize boarded.

The only hitch to their association was the unfortunate existence of John Bonney. Anne, however, set about solving this difficulty with characteristic enterprise by approaching her husband for a formal separation, offering to have Rackham pay him a liberal sum by way of compensation. It is very likely that John Bonney welcomed the arrangement. Anne had turned libertine on his hands and he had had little commerce with her since the day he surprised her lying in a hammock with another man.

But somehow the news reached the ear of the Governor of the island who took a different view of the matter. Summoning the parties concerned he gave them a piece of his mind together with the solemn promise that if he heard anything more about the proposed separation he would have Anne publicly flogged, and, what was more, Rackham himself would be obliged to wield the lash!

This edict set the couple back on their heels. Rackham, meanwhile, had squandered all his gold and now began to feel the pinch of an empty pocket; besides, life on shore was beginning to pall and he longed once again for the feel of a deck beneath his feet and the freedom of the blue Caribbean.

In Anne he found a kindred spirit. Between them they plotted secretly to seize a sloop which lay in the harbour and to run away to sea. Rackham had no difficulty in collecting a crew of ex-pirates who, like himself, were fed up of shore life and yearned to be back at the "sweet trade." He readily agreed to take Anne along, provided she adopted male attire (no new departure for her) and swore to keep her identity secret.

After some clever spying ably done by Anne, a date was fixed for the venture, the time midnight. Fortune was kind to the schemers, the night was dark and rainy, all hands were punctual, and with Anne Bonney back in man's disguise, the most resolute of the lot, they took a boat and rowed out to the sloop. Once on board, Anne, a cutlass in one hand, a pistol in the other, made straight for the ship's watch and silenced them effectively; Rackham and the others meanwhile hastily heaved in one cable and slipping the other drove down the harbour.

They had to pass the fort and guardship which hailed them, asking where they were going. Through the rain and fog Rackham called back that his cable had parted and there was nothing else on board but a grappling which would not hold them.

Shrouded by the darkness, he put out one small sail to give them steerage way, then, once past the harbour mouth, up to the sloop's tapering spars rose sail after sail as the trim vessel bounded out into the night and loud cheers broke from the throats of the pirate crew. It was on the deck of this sloop that the paths of the two women pirates at last converged and there, too, one of the strangest chapters of Jamaican history was destined to be written.

From that time on the name *Rackham* became the most dreaded in the Caribbean, his reputation and success being attributable in no small measure to the daring and prowess of his two female crew members who, although unaware of each other's secret, became close friends and always went into action side by side. This strange attraction eventually led to a mutual revelation of their real selves, for Anne, falling in love with Mary whom she took for a handsome young seaman, first told the other the secret of her sex. "Mary Read," says Captain Johnson, "knowing what she would be at, and being very sensible of her incapacity that way, was forced to come to a right understanding with her; and so, to the great disappointment of Anne Bonney, she let her know she was a woman also."

Rackham, meanwhile, noticing the growing intimacy between Anne and the young sailor, threatened to cut the latter's throat if the affair continued, thus forcing Mary to take him also into her confidence, which, to the end, he never betrayed.

Romance was to enter Mary Read's life once more before the curtain was rung down on her masquerading career. On their cruise the freebooters took and plundered a number of ships out of Jamaica on board one of which was "a young fellow of the most engaging behaviour" whom Rackham pressed into service aboard the sloop. It was not long before the newcomer had unwittingly won Mary's heart. They soon became messmates and close companions and Mary prepared her plans for making her true identity known to him. "When she found he had a friendship for her as a man," Johnson records, "she suffered the discovery to be made by carelessly showing her breasts, which were very white."

The days that followed were wildly happy for the couple. They pledged their troth to each other and lived as husband and wife. This, Mary later declared before a Jamaican court, she looked upon to be as good a marriage in conscience as if it had been done by a minister in church.

An unexpected turn of events, however, was soon to cast a shadow over their happiness and give Mary the chance to demonstrate the depth and selflessness of her devotion. It happened that the young seaman quarrelled one day with another crew member who challenged him to a duel. The sloop being at anchor off one of the islands, the two men appointed an hour when they should go ashore and settle their dispute, swords and pistols, pirate fashion.

Mary was frantic with anxiety when she learnt of the impending duel and determined to prevent it at all costs. Accordingly she took the first opportunity possible of starting a quarrel with the pirate and, challenging him ashore, fixed the time two hours earlier than that at which he should meet her lover.

Mary Read had fought many duels in her time, but never before from such a motive or with so fierce a determination to win. At the appointed time she and the pirate went ashore and together selected a secluded spot for their fight. Their exchange of fire resulted in no hits on either side and whipping out their cutlasses they began the duel to the death.

The pirate was heavier and stronger than Mary, but in her he found an adversary quick and agile who was able to parry or elude his every stroke. Back and forth across the beach they fought, their blades clashing with sharp staccato notes, their footsteps weaving the pattern of conflict in the soft white sands of the cay.

The pirate, heavier and slower than his opponent, began to tire first. Beads of sweat glistened on his hairy face and his breath now came with effort. Gradually through the haze of hate clouding his mind came the cold realisation that his antagonist was trifling with him, wearing him out against the instant when he should relax his guard . . .

Summoning all his strength he lunged at Mary in a fierce and desperate offensive, but the latter had danced beyond his reach whilst he, carried forward by the very savagery of the attack, lost his balance for a moment. He would no doubt have recovered but for his opponent who leapt to his side and in one quick motion tore open her rough sail-cloth shirt. For an instant only the pirate forgot his guard, forgot his peril as he stared in utter astonishment at what he saw. But that instant was his undoing, for Mary, grasping his sword arm, almost severed his head with a stroke of her cutlass. The pirate crumpled slowly sidewards to the ground and lay very still, a red foam bubbled from his lips, staining the white sands of the cay.

Suddenly Mary Read heard the familiar sound of a boat grounding on the beach; she looked up and a faint smile lit her features. It was her lover come in good time to keep his appointment with the pirate.

In the Public Record Office, London, is a rare pamphlet, printed in Jamaica in 1721 by Robert Baldwin who set up the island's first printing-press. The pamphlet is entitled in part:

THE TRYALS of Captain John Rackam, and other PIRATES . . . *Who were all Condemn'd for* PIRACY, *at the Town of St. Jago de la Vega, in the Ifland of* JAMAICA, *on Wednefday and Thurfday the Sixteenth and Seventeenth Days of November,* 1720.

AS ALSO, THE

TRYALS *of* Mary Read *and* Anne Bonny, *alias* Bonn,

. . . And of feveral Others, who were alfo condemn'd for PIRACY.

As the actual Admiralty Court records relating to the trial no longer exist, this pamphlet is of supreme importance for the story of the Woman Pirates. Nor can there be any question of its authenticity since it was sent to the Council of Trade in lieu of a written official report by the Governor, Sir Nicholas Lawes, who himself presided over the Court. It furnishes no information about the previous history of the Women Pirates beyond the description of them as "late of the Island of *Providence* Spinsters"; nor, on certain points, does it always support Captain Johnson's account, but this is doubtless explained by his own admission that he included "some particulars which were not so publicly known."

The "other PIRATES" of the pamphlet include Rackham's nine guests from the piragua. Lovat Fraser in his book *Pirates* (1921), says the judge, in passing sentence of death on them, made a "very pathetic speech, exhorting them to bear their sufferings patiently, assuring them that if they were innocent, which he very much doubted, then their reward would be greater in the Other World. But," adds Mr. Fraser, "everybody must own their case was very hard in this." The judge's speech is, unfortunately, not recorded in the Baldwin pamphlet.

Rackham was executed at Gallows Point on the Palisadoes, and his body gibbetted—as a grim warning to the piratically minded—on the sandy cay near Port Royal which bears his name to-day. It was known formerly as Deadman's Cay. On the morning of his execution he was allowed a visit from his sweetheart of happier days. The interview was short and disappointing for the condemned pirate chief, for the fiery Anne, still outraged at his conduct off Negril, had no word of consolation for him, nor did she conceal her disgust as she stared at the sorry figure of the fallen chieftain huddled in a corner of the condemned cell with the rest of his crew.

"I am sorry to see you here," she said, "but if you had fought like a man you would not now be hanged like a dog!"

When their sex was discovered in court, Anne Bonney and Mary Read were ordered a separate trial. This was held on the 28th November, 1720, over a week after Rackham and the rest had been hanged. The evidence mustered against the women pirates was heavy. It included the deposition of one Dorothy Thomas whose canoe was plundered by Rackham during his cruise along the north coast. She said that it was "the largenefs of their Breafts" which betrayed their real sex to her woman's eye, for otherwise they wore men's jackets and trousers, tied their heads with handkerchiefs and each carried a cutlass and pistol. She said they cursed and swore at the men to kill her to prevent her "coming against them" later.

Another witness, Thomas Dillon, master of a sloop taken by the pirates, said that Anne and Mary were both "very profligate, curfing and fwearing much, and very ready and willing to do any Thing on Board."

To these and other charges the women pirates offered nothing material by way of answer. They were found guilty, of course, and sentenced to death. But they doubtless listened to the sentence with equanimity for they still held the last trump in the pack. As soon as judgment was pronounced both women promptly informed the Court that they were pregnant and prayed that execution of the sentence might be stayed! An "inspection," ordered by the Court, later confirmed the truth of their plea and their sentence was accordingly respited.

Both cheated the gallows, in the end. Anne was eventually reprieved and disappears from recorded history, although it is believed that her father, through his connections with influential people in the island, arranged for her return to Carolina; while Mary died of a fever contracted during her lying-in. Her burial on the 28th April, 1721, is briefly recorded in the earliest Register of Burials for St. Catherine.

Mary's lover was acquitted as it was proved that he had been pressed into service aboard the pirate sloop. According to Captain Johnson, Mary herself might have earned the clemency of the Court but for one damning piece of evidence: at the trial it was disclosed that on being asked once what profit she could find in a life continually threatened by death from fire, sword, or hanging, she replied, that, "as to hanging, she thought it no great hardship, for, were it not for that, every cowardly fellow would turn Pirate, and so infest the seas that men of courage must starve!"

The King
agt
Lewis Hutchison

Guilty.

Be it Remembered unto this Co...
Wheies Fearon, Francis Dennis, Thomas
Richards John Milward, William Bry...
..mble, Abraham Brinkley, Lachlin E...
Ryles Bentley and John Clifford goo...
midésseg then and there returned
behalf of our said Sovereign Lord the
And the said Jurors for our s...
do present and say that Lewis

The King against Lewis Hutchison

The Mad Master of Edinburgh Castle

IN THE PEDRO district of St. Ann, on a low hill near what used to be the main road running from St. Ann's Bay to the south side of the island, the ruins of Edinburgh Castle still stand.

Built more than two hundred years ago, it was—in spite of its lofty title—a small, two-storied, square, stone building with two circular loop-holed towers placed at diagonally opposite corners. It had a door at one side of the front angle and another near the front tower on the east side. Traces remain of a fireplace on both stories of the front tower and of a series of sinister spiral steps in the back. Ruins adjacent to the Castle to the west are believed to have been the slave quarters.

Comparatively few people have heard or read of Edinburgh

The Mad Master of Edinburgh Castle

Castle and its infamous occupant; fewer, perhaps, have seen its crumbling ruins. The road no longer winds close to the little fortress with its well-placed loop-holes, calm and quiet reign over the property and on the green slope before the Castle fat cattle graze placidly, for the evil reputation of the place and the memory of Lewis Hutchison, the homicidal maniac who lived there, have all but faded. And yet, in the island's Rogue's Gallery, Hutchison towers above all comers in evil and daring. Bandit, desperado and murderer, he was the most feared and hated man of his day and (according to contemporary opinion) "the most detestable and abandoned villain that ever disgraced the human species."

His sins, upon which his reputation rests, are fully recorded, but not much else for certain. Accounts differ widely and are often impossible to reconcile. It is generally agreed, however, that he was born in Scotland in 1733 and studied medicine there for some time. He seems to have acquired his Pedro property legally enough, but the fine herd of cattle with which it was soon stocked is said to have consisted largely of strays from neighbouring pens.

Official records, preserved in the Jamaica Archives, shed their quota of light on Hutchison's activities and help to fill out the story of this extraordinary man. In the St. Ann *Vestry Orders*, for example, under date 28th February, 1769 (and other dates as well) his name appears on the "List of persons the Justices & Vestry have . . . recorded as fit to serve as Jurors." Included on the list also is a certain *Jonathan Hutton Practitioner in Physick and Surgery*. Two years later we find Hutchison being called upon to supply slave labour for mending the road passing Edinburgh Castle to Pedro River. Then there are the records of his trial for murder "at a Supreme Court of Judicature held at the Town of Saint Jago de la Vega in the County of Middlesex . . . on the last Tuesday in ffebruary . . . in the Year of our Lord One thousand seven hundred and feventy three." In the same year the estate of Lewis Hutchison is returned at 93 head of stock and 24 slaves— but this is the end of the story, and in between those dates and scanty references lie all the incredible incidents of his life, many of which did not find their way into official archives.

Perhaps the best known account of Hutchison is given in *The Annals of Jamaica* by the Rev. George Wilson Bridges, based, it is said, on information obtained from a slave who related the facts as they were then current among the slaves in the district. A later account, written in 1879, by a descendant of the same Dr. Jonathan Hutton of the Jury List, one of the most prominent actors in the drama as we shall see, complements the former. Bridges who was rector of St. Ann from 1823 to 1837 was much moved by Hutchison's crimes and told the story in vivid detail and in language which as an echo of the "tone of the time" is worth repeating—

"In the close and wood-bound vale of Pedro, situated in the parish of Saint Ann, and nearly in the centre of the island, stood a small and lonely turret, dignified by its northern architect with the name of Edinburgh Castle. It commanded the only pass leading directly from the south side of the island to the north: the defile is scarcely an hundred yards across: and the mountains which inclose the solitary vale, arise on either side to an almost Alpine height.

"On this spot, which might have been selected for a new Thermopylae, there dwelt a wretch whose birth disgraced the 'land of the mountain and the flood:'—his name was Hutchinson—he possessed a few negroes, acquired a small property, and first stocked it with the strayed or stolen cattle of his neighbours.

"His slaves were the participators of his crimes; they were recently from Africa; their native habits were familiarised with the sight of blood; and their mistaken sense of duty, if not their characteristic cruelty, taught them silence and submission, though the dark and midnight crime of assassination stains not the nature of the unprovoked African.

"Yet no traveller who attempted that defile, however poor or wretched he might be, ever escaped the confines of their owner's narrow territory. The needy wanderer would sometimes call for refreshment at the only habitation which for many miles had cheered his weary eye, but it was the last he was destined ever to behold. The wealthy passenger was alike the mark and victim of his unerring aim, from a loophole under which he was compelled to pass. A thick-set hedge of logwood had also been so prepared by the road-side, at a short distance from the house, that while he could detain in conversation any one who might pass during the time that he was engaged in his cattle-fold hard by, his slaves from behind the fence could leisurely take aim at the devoted victim.

"It was not, however, money which the murderer thus sought. A savage disposition, wrought perhaps by some injury inflicted on him in early life, an unnatural detestation of the human race, could be gratified only by the sight of blood, and the contemplation of human agony; for if his destined victim were infirm, or sick, he carefully revived his strength; or if he could behold him first in fancied security, in a convivial assembly, or perhaps happy in the bosom of his family, it gave him greater satisfaction to inflict the blow which cut him off, and increased his appetite to relish the expiring struggle.

"To enjoy the gory spectacle, he first dissevered the ghastly head from the palpitating body: his most pleasing occupation was to whet his streaming knife; the gloomy temper of his soul was sated only by a copious flow of blood; and when he could no longer gaze upon the decaying countenance, he placed it high in the air, in the hollow trunk of a cotton tree, where vultures might complete the horrid deed. The mangled carcass was thrown down one of those deep and hollow drains which are peculiar to mountainous countries of volcanic origin, and whose mouths, descending perpendicularly, conduct the torrents which periodically fall to the level of the ocean.

"Nor were his crimes for many years suspected, though his society was shunned; so artfully did he contrive to conceal a character which otherwise might have been charitably pronounced insane. Justice, however, was at length gratified by the punishment of the guilty monster . . ." but not quite in the way Mr. Bridges records it, so here we part company for a time.

The age of concentration camps and the atom bomb can in some respects be more charitable than the age of the Rev. Mr. Bridges and would dispassionately pronounce Lewis Hutchison insane. The fact seems clear from the rector's own account: he himself comes close to the root of the matter in his reference to the warping influence of an injury inflicted on Hutchison in early life. He appears to have grown up in an atmosphere of strife and there are references to a savage feud that existed between the Hutchisons and a neighbouring family when he was a young man in Scotland which might have helped to change his character as it did the course of his life. There is also a theory that Hutchison had been jilted by "some 'lady fair' . . . which enraged him, unjustly, against all males." "Since all men's hands are against me, henceforth my hand will be against all men," he is said to have sworn, doubtless from the depths of a warped and injured mind. That he fulfilled his vow and squared accounts with mankind in the most appalling manner ever recorded in Jamaica, the Rev. Mr. Bridges has ably shown. Fortunately his career was fairly short and "Justice at length was gratified." The Manuscript of 1879 describes the events (not recorded in *The Annals*) that led to Hutchison's downfall.

Not far from Edinburgh Castle was a property named Bonneville Pen (or Hutton Bonvil, as it was then called) which, together with the adjoining property Lebanon Pen, was owned by Dr. Jonathan Hutton, a retired naval doctor of Lincolnshire, England. The time was about 1768, a short time since the arrival of Lewis Hutchison in the island, but already he had become the cause of much speculation and concern. The increasing number of cases of white travellers in the district disappearing without leaving a single trace was giving rise to alarm, while the persistent rumour linking the master of Edinburgh Castle with these disappearances was fast becoming a conviction. So unsettled was the state of the island, however, and so strong the fear the name of Hutchison already inspired, that harassed officials used every pretext for filing the reports away and turning deaf ears to the disturbing rumours.

Dr. Hutton himself spent a good deal of his time in England, and so had little occasion to come into contact with his unsavoury neighbour. The only time that he did ended disastrously. It came about as the result of a boundary dispute. Such disputes were common at that period largely because the business of conveyancing had been rather informally practised, and also because few of the boundaries had originally been run by surveyors. Hutchison, as was his custom, had taken the law into his own hands and laid claim to certain lands which Dr. Hutton insisted was his property. Enraged by Hutton's opposition Hutchison brooded on revenge. His opportunity was not long in coming.

One evening as the doctor, who was colonel of militia for St. Ann, was riding home from muster at Moneague with his Negro servant following some distance behind on foot, carrying his sabre and other accoutrements, Hutchison overhauled the man and took the sabre away from him saying, "You can give my compliments to Dr. Hutton and tell him I have got his sabre."

The doctor, we are certain, was a man of courage, but prudent withal, for, we read, he ignored the incident. Besides, there were no doubt more weighty matters to be seen to, including the arrangements for a trip to England with his wife and eight-year-old daughter Mary.

Mrs. Hutton, as previously arranged, left Bonneville ahead of the others for she had a visit to pay in neighbouring Clarendon parish before going on to Kingston to join her husband. All went according to plan and on the day arranged Dr. Hutton set out early on horseback, his daughter riding with a servant, accompanied by a retinue of his staff, on the long journey to Kingston and the waiting packet boat.

"Dr. Hutton," says the Manuscript, "intended to pursue the route now usually taken from Pedro through Moneague and

St. Thomas-ye-Vale to Spanish Town, and on to Kingston, with this exception that the public road from Pedro to Moneague in those days lay across the hill from Grier Park, where they were met by Hutchison and a following of his slaves. He rode up to Dr. Hutton, who was unarmed, and attacked him fiercely, the weapon he used being Dr. Hutton's own sabre which he had stolen. He struck the doctor such a severe blow on the head with this sabre that the latter fell senseless from his horse. Hutchison made off with his servants, and Dr. Hutton's terrified servants carried him back to Bonneville, where he stayed for a few days until he partially recovered, when, without venturing to travel by the same road he had at first intended to take, his servants took him across the hills to join his wife in Clarendon and they and their little girl went on to Kingston together. Dr. Hutton laid information there about Hutchison; but as he was unable through the cruel blow he had received to remain in the Island to prosecute the matter, no steps appeared to have been taken. Dr. Hutton proceeded to England still suffering much from the wound in his head, and when he got there had to undergo the operation of trepanning, and wore a silver plate in his head until the day of his death."

It was more than a year before he returned to Jamaica, but the lapse of time had not lessened his determination to bring Hutchison to justice. He was soon to discover, however, that the same time had so added to the murderer's reputation that although the authorities were now disposed to make a move in the matter, they could find no one who would venture into dread Edinburgh Castle and serve the warrant on its mad master!

Eventually a young English soldier named John Callendar volunteered to go and with a party of friends set out on his mission, but "as soon as Hutchison found what was their errand, he fired at Callendar and shot him dead on the spot. The others fled, and Hutchinson was again left unmolested."

Secure behind his loop-holed walls and the equally effective ramparts his dreaded reputation had raised up around him, Lewis Hutchison contemplated the balance sheet of his life that night with satisfaction. "Henceforth my hand will be against all men"—how well he had fulfilled his vow! Mankind had paid, but now the account was closed, for now he had gone too far. The reports of frightened Negro slaves might be disregarded, but not the sworn testimony of a dozen white witnesses. The angry tide of public indignation was now at full flow, a tide destined to break with force against the evil castle and sweep its mad master to his doom.

According to the Manuscript of 1879, a strong and well-armed party set out for Edinburgh Castle, stormed it and captured Hutchison, but here the account is in error, and perhaps better so for this would have been a dull pale end to a career that had never lacked colour. So here we part company with the later writer and listen again to the Rev. Mr. Bridges—

With almost the whole island aroused and in full cry, Hutchison abandoned his fortress, escaped south to Old Harbour and there put to sea in an open boat in a bold attempt to board a vessel then off the coast. But the dragnet had been well cast: the very sea and coasts were being watched by units of the Royal Navy under no less a commander than Admiral Rodney whose *Formidable* was even then in port. The vessel which Hutchison managed to reach was intercepted by one of the Admiral's officers, George Turnbull.

Cornered now, Hutchison made one last despairing effort to escape—or, if that failed, to take his own life—by leaping overboard. But in this too he was thwarted for, we are told, his flaming red hair betrayed his presence even when he dived and he was eventually rescued by men from the warship, taken into port and later sent on to Spanish Town for trial.

Rodney received the official thanks of the House of Assembly for his "ready and effectual assistance of the civil power, at the instance of his Majesty's Attorney-General, in apprehending Lewis Hutchison." The House also voted Turnbull £50 to be laid out in the purchase of a gold-hilted sword, and desired

Rodney "to signify to the proper department of state, the sense the House entertains of Mr. Turnbull's merit."

Captured at last and safely lodged behind bars, legal proceedings against Hutchison commenced. His house was searched and there quantities of clothing believed to have been the property of his victims discovered. From the dark corners of the archives came the official documents with their indictments of the murderer. His slaves, no longer silenced by submission or fear, bore testimony against him, telling tale after tale of "dark and midnight crimes"; of the sink-hole near the Castle—his "unfathomable charnel-house"—which had received the mangled bodies of their master's victims and kept his secrets well. True tales no doubt, exciting to the popular fancy, but almost useless in a court of law since the evidence of coloured people then was seldom admitted. So Lewis Hutchison was put on trial for one crime only—"the Murther of John Callendar."

In the proceedings that followed, however, the truth of these other reports was largely substantiated; while even more startling was the revelation that Hutchison was not alone, but had gathered around him a group of perverts like himself who now found themselves as deeply and criminally involved as their friend!

Resulting from an inquest held at Hutchison's house, a planter named James Walker was tried, found guilty and condemned to death for murdering a yeoman named William Lickley with his sword.

Another case of murder at Edinburgh Castle involving others besides Hutchison, the investigation of which produced most surprising results, concerned "one Timothy Cronin late Schoolmaster to Roger Maddix," whose dead body was among those disposed of down the hole. The information was laid this time by one of Hutchison's slaves named Hector who told the investigators that he and another slave called Harry belonging to John Maddix, were ordered by their masters (being primed as well by the promise of a three-pistole reward) to strangle Cronin while pinioned in

Hutchison's stocks and then to throw the body into the hole.

The story of this murder seems to have leaked out and Hutchison, growing alarmed at the reports that began to circulate, got Hector with a good deal of difficulty—and no doubt, fear and trembling on the slave's part!—to go down into the hole and recover the remains of the schoolmaster which were later buried in a spot on the property chosen by Hutchison. The investigators were taken to the burial place by Hector where human remains were exhumed which, on careful examination, the investigators declared they "verily believed" to be those of the unfortunate Cronin.

An index of the Belsen-like orgies that took place at Edinburgh Castle is furnished by the slave's sworn statement that the murder was watched by an enthusiastic audience which, beside Hutchison and Roger Maddix, included the latter's wife, Dorcas, as well as a Susanna Cole and a certain Miss Elizabeth Thomas in whose possession Cronin's watch and seal were later found! This discovery led to her arrest and trial for the murder, the allegation being that she "did Choake and ftrangle" the schoolmaster with "a certain linnen Handkerchief of the Value of feven pence halfpenny Current Money of Jamaica." She pleaded not guilty, was so found by the jury and acquitted.

Hutchison also pleaded "in no wise guilty" to the charge brought against him, but in his case the issue was otherwise. He was tried, convicted and hanged in Spanish Town on the 16th of March, 1773. It is reported that he was defended by the most eminent counsel in the island at the time, and that he behaved with the greatest insolence from his commitment to the moment of his execution.

"The enormity of his crimes," concludes Mr. Bridges, "might be exceeded by his hardened insolence before his judges; but his reckless gaze upon the instrument which was to convey him before the tribunal of his Maker, finds no parallel in the history of crime or punishment: nor can the annals of human depravity equal the fact that, at the foot of the scaffold, he left an hundred pounds in gold to erect a monument, and to inscribe the marble with a record of his death."

The inscription, composed by Hutchison himself but never carved on stone, was:

Lewis Hutchison—hanged in Spanish Town, Jamaica, on the sixteenth morning of March, in the year of *his* Lord one thousand seven hundred and seventy-three.— Aged forty years.

> *Their sentence, pride and malice, I defy;*
> *Despise their power, and, like a Roman, die.*

Mistress of the Jamaican Revels

"THE FEMALE ART of getting rich in Jamaica," declared Sir Nicholas Lawes, "is predicated on two short rules—*marry* and *bury*!" Sir Nicholas, governor of the island in the spacious early years of the eighteenth century, could speak with some authority, although he was unjust in describing the art as a purely feminine one, since he himself married successively five widows of considerable means.

A far more striking exponent of the art, however, was the notorious Teresa Constantia Phillips, the self-styled Pride of England who became the five-times-married Mistress of the Jamaican Revels.

She attracted the notice, if not the sympathy, of men like Horace Walpole who likened her in his *Letters* to Thaïs, Fredegonde and the Czarina; and of Fielding who coupled her with Jezebel, Delilah and Joan of Naples. *Hussy!* people hissed behind her back, *Bluebeard, harlot!* But others thought her lovely, fascinating, desirable. And, indeed, she was all these things and more: she was the greatest beauty of her day and one of the most colourful characters of all time.

In her *Apology for the Conduct of Mrs. Teresa Constantia Phillips*, a three-volume work typical of the "Blackmail Books" of the period, published in 1748, going through four editions, the notorious lady tells a good deal about her life and escapades which were to have earned her the reputation she so justly enjoyed. Its publication caused a considerable stir at the time and brought the author some notoriety, although the financial returns were disappointing—a fact which no doubt helped shape the events that were to take her eventually to Jamaica.

From a brief account of her life we gather that she was born at West Chester about 1708, the daughter of an army officer in poor circumstances, and educated in London. At the age of thirteen she was seduced by "Thomas Grimes" (the future fourth Earl of Chesterfield). A year later to avoid arrest for debt she went through a Fleet form of marriage with a Mr. Francis Devall (or Delafield) whom she had never seen before and with whom she never exchanged a word. These clandestine marriages were performed by needy chaplains, without banns or licence, in London's Fleet Prison. As many as thirty such marriages were performed in a day, and in the four months ending with 12th February, 1705, a record number of 2,954 was registered. The practice was eventually suppressed in 1774.

Despite a career of fashionable dissipation and a succession of amours "as public as Charing Cross," a rather well-to-do if dull Dutch merchant named Henry Muilman fell under her spell and she found herself being courted for wife. They were married on the 9th February, 1723, but the venture proved a failure. Most of the *Apology*, in fact, is clouded with lamentations over this marriage and the way Muilman treated her. He did eventually obtain an annulment, but was generous enough as to allow her an annuity of £200 which, however, her outrageous conduct soon lost her.

She first came out to Jamaica in 1738, travelling under the so-called "protecting companionship" of a wealthy landowner and Assemblyman named Nedham. Details of her first stay in the island are scanty. She appears to have spent most of her time in the parishes of Portland and St. Thomas-in-the-Vale, probably working on her *Apology*, until 1741 when she went back to England to see to its publication.

It was in 1754 that she returned to settle in Jamaica, although she did not settle down; peace and quiet were not for "Con" Phillips; to her, gaiety and excitement were the breath of existence and the social life of the colony was soon to quiver to the impact of her personality.

It was not inappropriate, perhaps, that shortly after her arrival the island was torn by a controversy which almost ended in civil war, a controversy in which, as we would expect, the redoubtable "Con" Phillips played her part. The cause of the trouble was the transfer of the capital from Spanish Town to Kingston.

It may seem strange to day that any other town could be preferred to Kingston as the seat of government, but in the middle of the eighteenth century the position was rather different. Kingston was then only fifty years old, while Spanish Town—the *Villa de la Vega* of the Spaniards—had been a capital for more than two hundred and thirty years! Even so the upstart Kingston had a good case. In its brief half century it had become the seat of trade and the richest town in Jamaica. It enjoyed the blessings of a capital, contended one historian: "beauty, safety and wealth; order, plenty, public amusements and commercial occupations."

These, no doubt, were some of the considerations which weighed with the then governor, Admiral Charles Knowles, but there were others. He had long been a good friend to the town which, among other services, he had efficiently fortified. But his earlier benefits were small compared with the one he proposed to confer in constituting it the seat of government.

The proposal was, of course, strongly supported by Kingston and the eastern parishes and as strenuously opposed by Spanish Town and the western parishes. Partisan feeling ran high; cries of jobbery and corruption, intimidation and despotism echoed in council chambers and taverns. The Assembly twice rejected the bill authorising the removal, but Knowles was determined to have his way, and it was passed eventually by the third House he convened in which he had succeeded in gaining a corrupt majority "garbled by very iniquitous and illegal practices." On the 7th May a satisfied Knowles gave his formal assent to the bill for the removal of the capital. It is an interesting commentary on the times that one of the reasons urged in opposition to the removal was that the gay life of Kingston "would be destructive of the morals" of Assemblymen—an argument which must have amused "Con" Phillips.

While petitions were being hurriedly drawn up and rushed to England praying that the bill might be disallowed, steps were being taken to carry it into effect. The archives were moved to Kingston and the superior courts established there. As it was, the bill had not actually been sanctioned by the King, but Knowles had left the island before this was known.

He was succeeded as governor by Henry Moore who on the 3rd October 1758, announced the disallowance of the law and so brought Kingston's short and glittering reign as the capital city to an end. Immediately the machinery went into reverse gear. Four days after the proclamation thirty wagon loads of archives filed out of Kingston on their way to the old capital under an armed escort.

Mistress of the Jamaican Revels

When the cavalcade arrived Spanish Town went delirious with joy. Flags and banners were hoisted, splendid entertainments arranged and, that evening, the illuminations and firework displays transformed the dark tropical night to day. The *pièce de résistance* was the burning in effigy of Admiral Knowles and his ship H.M.S. *Cornwall*. This last bit of exuberance was not perhaps in the best taste, and the *Kingston Journal*, a newspaper only two years old at the time, was prompt to point this out in a pungent article. The burning in effigy of Knowles was bad enough, it observed, but the burning of the *Cornwall* was an insult to the King whose ship she was, and the flag which had been so ignominiously struck was that of the British nation. Moreover, the paper concluded, such conduct was not calculated to restore peace and goodwill to the distracted community.

The House of Assembly, rubbed raw by recent events, was angered by the article and ordered the paper's printer, Thomas Woolhead, into custody. Woolhead, terrified for his own safety, disclaimed all responsibility. The author of the article, he declared, was a lady—Teresa Constantia Phillips.

It is difficult to know what effect this disclosure had on the Honourable House, although we may well imagine. The lady was someone to reckon with. Still an intimate friend of Nedham, himself a one-time Assemblyman and member of the Council, she was also very popular with the pleasure-loving Governor who had recently appointed her his Mistress of the Revels.

History does not reveal what influences finally swayed the Honourable House, but we know the action taken. Old Woolhead, the nervous newspaperman, was released and "Con" Phillips taken into custody—a gesture only, to be sure, since she was almost immediately released. And the matter was at an end.

As Mistress of the Revels—the post to which Henry Moore had appointed Teresa—her duties included authority over theatrical performances and the direction of all balls and entertainments given by the Governor. The office, incidentally, had no counterpart in the Northern Colonies and was in itself an indication of the high times and merry hearts peculiar to this period of Jamaica's history.

Teresa was ideally suited to the post and the post suited her well. Privileges attaching to it included, in addition to the measure of control over the players and their productions already mentioned, a seat on the stage at every theatrical performance and a benefit of one hundred guineas each season. As there were two seasons a year this represented a handsome perquisite.

Already twice married she was by no means disillusioned with the institution and, in fact, determined to try it for a third time. Her first Jamaican husband was a prosperous Irish land-surveyor of Kingston named Hugh Montgomery. Their early years together passed uneventfully enough when for no apparent reason Montgomery began to lose weight. From a healthy, robust man he became a sickly, emaciated invalid, a puzzle to his physicians and friends alike, although there was a general feeling that concern over his wife's carryings-on might be at the root of his distemper.

As time went on he grew steadily weaker until his friends with commendable tact, courage and foresight ventured to suggest that the time had arrived when he ought to think seriously about the disposal of his worldly goods. He yielded to their promptings, and doubtless to influence from the same quarter also, by cutting Teresa completely from his will. But in this he and his friends had reckoned without the good lady.

Hoping that a change of air and scenery might succeed where other methods had failed, the doctors recommended a trip to the country for the ailing surveyor, to which he readily agreed. Teresa too felt that a change in the country might help, but seemed grieved at the prospect of the separation (she, of course, was too busy with her Revel duties to accompany her husband) and quite inconsolable when the day of parting arrived, her sorrow knowing no bounds at the sight of the chaise which was to take her husband away from her.

On the front steps of their home Hugh Montgomery paused to kiss his tearful wife good-bye. She clung desperately to him, pouring forth her grief in impassioned speech: she would miss him so much when he was gone—their life together had been so happy—she had always loved him, been a dutiful and affectionate wife to him—and now they were to be separated, perhaps, perhaps for ever—!

This raised the question of her future security, should the worst happen. Had he made a will, she inquired delicately, and if so, had he provided for her?

It took some effort for the surveyor to struggle free of her embrace. Yes, he had made his will, he assured her, and had made ample provision in it for his true and loving wife. With this assurance he gave her a parting kiss on the forehead and turned hastily towards the waiting chaise. He had barely taken a step, however, when a heavy hand grasped him by the collar of his coat and jerked him round and he found himself staring into his wife's narrowed blue eyes as she shook a document under his nose which he instantly recognised as *the will*! In the hurry of packing he must have forgotten it in the pocket of another pair of breeches which Teresa had industriously searched.

"What the devil do you mean by saying you have provided for me in your will?" she snapped. "Look at this—you haven't left me a farthing!"

Montgomery began to perspire profusely. The tight grip on his collar made breathing difficult and a cold sick feeling began to creep up inside him. One thing was clear to him: there was no use trying to deny the imposture; he must simply make amends as best he might.

"I—I was a fool when I made that will," he explained, lamely. "I didn't realise how true a wife you were, how much you meant to me, until now. Teresa, this is what I shall do, I shall make another will as you dictate . . ."

"That you shall certainly do," she interrupted, "here and now!"

Montgomery was rudely pulled indoors and dumped down on a chair before his writing desk on which, in readiness, was pen, paper and sealing wax. Three men, Teresa's friends, we may assume (their names survive on the document) had appeared, it seemed to the bewildered Montgomery, from nowhere, ready to witness the signing, sealing, publishing and declaring of his will . . .

That will, made on the 14th January, 1760, may be seen to this day in the Island Record Office, Spanish Town. It is a very brief document, eloquent in its simplicity and singleness of purpose. "Before the infirmities of age impair the facultys of my mind," wrote the ailing Montgomery, "I make and declare this to be my last Will and Testament not knowing that in my life I ever made another. In the first place after my legal debts and funeral expenses are paid I leave and bequeath all the rest residue and remainder of my Estate both real and personal of whatsoever kind it may be both here and in Ireland unto my dear and well beloved wife Teresa Constantia Montgomery and constitute and appoint her my sole Executrix and Heiress to every thing I shall die seized of."

Montgomery had no choice. In his weakened state he was no match for his robust spouse. Teresa stood at the front door and watched the chaise until it was out of sight, a sinister smile playing about her full red lips. A few days later Hugh Montgomery was dead.

A year had barely passed before Teresa was married again, this time to a young Scotsman of the city named Samuel Callendar, Commissary for the French prisoners of war brought to the island.

Callendar came of a good family, was well respected and occupied a prominent position in the social life of the colony —that is, until he married Teresa. Soon after the wedding a remarkable change took place: he dropped completely out of the social stream, is said to have been seen outside of his home no oftener than three times during his two years of married life, and was dead before the second year had passed!

Once again Teresa found herself amply provided for. Callendar had died intestate so she assumed the administration of his affairs and became heir to all his possessions, including a cargo worth some £2,000 which arrived shortly after his death consigned to him. This spelt "Easy-Street" for the Mistress of the Revels who immediately blossomed forth in a rich new chariot.

On the 24th of April, 1762, Teresa and a certain Monsieur Adhamar de Lantagnac were "Joyn'd together in Holy Matrimony" in the Parish Church of Kingston. Adhamar had only recently arrived in the island among a batch of French prisoners over whom Teresa's late husband had control. He had grown up among the Canadian Indians whose customs and habits he had adopted, including even the barbaric tattoo marks with which his body, legs and arms were embellished. He was an immediate sensation in Kingston social circles and Teresa recognised in him the ideal consort for her sensational self. He was an exciting, colourful personality, a *bon vivant* and lavish spender—especially when spending someone else's money.

For a time Teresa's fortune furnished the fuel for the gay, fast pace set by herself and the Frenchman, but her resources were not inexhaustible, nor were they being mended by any form of income. She soon perceived that *monsieur* was more of an embarrassment than an ornament. He refused to do anything but eat, drink and dress, which was bad enough, but, what was worse, she had begun to tire of him So Monsieur de Lantagnac was handed his marching orders and we last hear of him leaving for Hispaniola (or Martinique, the accounts are conflicting) as he disappears from history.

Teresa was in her fifties at this time. With the inevitable fading of her great beauty, her fortunes also began to decline. She did not marry again—perhaps suitors were now more difficult to come by—but she could not abandon the life of revelry to which she was dedicated.

As her fortune dwindled she began to borrow heavily. When her creditors grew restive she temporised. One day her carriage and horses were seized for debt. She wrote little urgent notes on scented paper to her friends. They rallied round and soon she was driving in her chariot again, but not for long. Once more her creditors levied, once more her friends came to the rescue. A third time it happened, with the same result, but she was running short of friends, as she had run short of cash, and when her creditors foreclosed a fourth time there was no one to redeem her.

The Mistress of the Revels who had watched the curtain fall so often at the Kingston Theatre marking the end of yet another performance, could not believe that now her own show was over. Where were her friends, she asked, where was her wealth? It was all very baffling.

On her deathbed she lay, still struggling with a situation she could not understand. She called for a mirror. Someone, perhaps an old faithful slave, gave it to her. She studied her features carefully, stunned by the testimony of her own eyes.

"Alas, what is beauty!" she cried. "I who was once the Pride of England am become an ugly object."

It is said that she made them set the mirror up at the foot of her bed so that she might see herself to the end, altered as she was, and reflect on the last deceits of death against which she had raised no defence in life.

Now that the end was so close she began to be troubled by the fear that her corpse might be arrested for her debts on its way to the grave—a common custom at that time. Her last and dearest wish was that she might die on a Saturday night, so that being buried on a Sunday her body would not be molested. Her wish was granted. She was conscious to the last and is said to have expressed great satisfaction since she had reason to suspect that a certain apothecary would not otherwise have suffered her body to go to its grave in peace.

But who the apothecary was remained her last of many secrets.

She died in Kingston and was buried in the churchyard on the 20th January, 1765. Her funeral was a solitary one. She had no friends left, there was nobody—not even the apothecary—to mourn or mock the Mistress of the Jamaican Revels who was once the Pride of England as her body went unnoticed to its nameless grave.

The Case of the Counterfeit Doubloons

NATHANIEL HAWTHORNE the well-known American author, is perhaps best remembered for his novel *The Scarlet Letter*. In the opening chapter the writer tells us that he found the material for the story in an ancient document while poking and burrowing into the heaped-up rubbish of a large room on the second floor of the Custom-house at Salem.

The idea of the story being found in an old loft, says the Introduction, is of course, imaginary. The author, however, while admitting that he allowed himself much licence in embellishing the tale and in "imagining the motives and modes of passion that influenced the characters who figure in it," declares, nevertheless, that what he contends for is the "authenticity of the outline."

The Case of the Counterfeit Doubloons

Before devoting himself entirely to authorship Mr. Hawthorne was attached to the American Civil Service both in his own country and abroad. It was, in fact, at a dinner given in his honour at Liverpool where he was then the United States consul that, we are told, the Honourable George Cuthbert, who administered the Government of Jamaica in 1832 and again in 1834, related a strange story of old Jamaica, a story which, it is said, interested Mr. Hawthorne immensely.

In its barest outline *The Scarlet Letter* is the story of a young clergyman who committed himself with a beautiful young girl for which sin the couple suffered due punishment, the "offspring of their guilt"—a girl child—becoming in time a lady of quality and "the richest heiress of her day in the New World."

The story which the Honourable George Cuthbert related at that dinner in Liverpool was also the story of a young clergyman and a beautiful girl, the story of a great sin and its wages—a story I have called *The Case of the Counterfeit Doubloons*.

I have sometimes wondered if the Honourable George Cuthbert really believed in his after-dinner story, or if he, too, regarded it as a beguiling legend: for it is odd how soon the story came to be so treated; odd also was the way in which popular speculation concerning a certain tombstone in the churchyard of the Kingston Parish Church soon became an accepted part of the strange story. Let us trace these two odd developments from the various accounts of the story which appeared *in print*.

Although of relatively recent date, we might begin with that published in the December 1913 issue of a local periodical called *Plummer's Magazine*, for this is the fullest version I have found:

"Under a plain slate slab," says the writer, "near the entrance of the North transept of the Parish Church, Kingston, lie the remains of the unfortunate clergyman who was under painful circumstances found guilty of coining counterfeit doubloons and paid the death penalty in Kingston Parade.

"Tradition says a young Curate residing in Spanish Town, but who was at the time acting Rector of Kingston, fell in love with the beautiful daughter of a city merchant. The young lady recognised to be fair and beautiful was the light of her father's home but she was the descendant of a slave and was of negro origin which lent her that tint to her colour which made her beautiful."

Clergymen (the writer continues) had *carte blanche* at that time to the houses of families in the Parish, and soon the young curate became a frequent visitor to the girl's home for they had fallen deeply, fatally in love. So secretly did they order their affairs, however, that the liaison was never suspected, and even when the girl was found to be pregnant no shadow of suspicion fell on the clergyman.

The merchant's grief on the discovery of his daughter's condition was irrepressible, nor were matters improved by the girl's staunch refusal to disclose the identity of her lover. Distressed by the affair and pressed at the same time by grave business difficulties, he committed suicide. The consequences of his rash act were worse than he could have imagined. His estate and personal effects were taken over and, along with his other goods and chattels, his daughter was put up for sale at public auction.

The curate meanwhile, desperate at this sudden, tragic turn of events, began to explore every possible means of raising sufficient money to buy the girl who was soon to bear his child, but it was an impossible feat. As the auction day drew closer, in desperation he hit on the reckless scheme of making counterfeit money, his knowledge of chemistry standing him in good stead as he worked feverishly behind the closed doors of the church vestry.

For a time it seemed as though his daring shift might succeed, but his good fortune was short-lived. One day in his anxiety he spoilt one of the coins which he rashly passed out with the others. The counterfeit was discovered, his house was searched and his guilt confirmed. He was arrested, brought to trial, convicted, sentenced to death and hanged for the crime on the Kingston Parade, opposite the church he had defiled!

As for the girl who shared much of his guilt, the rest of her story has all the glitter and charm of a fairy tale. The writer tells us that she was auctioned for a "fabulous price" to another city merchant; that she became a "lady of fashion in Kingston and St. Andrew"; that her daughter grew up to be a beautiful girl, was married to a young Englishman of note, recently arrived in the island, who, not two years after the marriage, succeeded to a baronetcy "and is to-day the progenitor of a distinguished and very wealthy family in the English Aristocracy."

The writer records the fact that the Honourable George Cuthbert related the story at the dinner in Liverpool for Nathaniel Hawthorne, and that the publication of Hawthorne's *Scarlet Letter* "revived the story of the curate and the girl." Finally he mentions the name of a Kingston solicitor who, at that time, possessed the counterfeit doubloon—a Carol III— which betrayed the curate, and who had often refused large sums of money for it.

Notice two points about this account: the writer credits the story of the curate and the girl to "tradition," but begins with the statement that the clergyman was buried "under a plain slate slab" in the churchyard of the Kingston Parish Church. It is strange that he should have made this claim for by 1913 the myth of the *"plain slab"* had long been exploded. How did the myth start in the first place? To discover this we must go back some two hundred years or more into the city's past, for it was about then that a new stone monument seems to have made its appearance—or first began to be remarked—among the other tombs in the churchyard at the principal entrance to the north transept of the Parish Church. It was a large, dark blue slate slab, not very unlike a number of others nearby, except in one respect —it had no inscription on its polished surface: it had, in fact, been laid face down!

To-day that stone is old and footworn, but two centuries back it was new and smooth; to-day we know its secret, but its mystery was deep and unexplored two hundred years ago. Generations of churchgoers during that long spell of time saw the slab. They must have wondered about it. We know they walked on it, countless numbers of them, for their shoes have worn it smooth. But how many probed its secret, how many solved the riddle of its stony silence?

Time, wrote Lovat Fraser, though a good Collector is not always a reliable Historian. So it was in time that a strange story sprang up about the stone, a story slow of growth at first, whispered casually, doubtfully in the beginning, then gaining strength and spreading by degrees. Now the parishioners who filed into the churchyard of a Sunday morning had a tale to tell about the monument, a beguiling tale which Time, the good Collector, had patiently gathered.

Soon the story found its way into publications of the period. The *Jamaica Almanack* for 1879/80, for example, carries this terse account:

> Just at the main entrance into the Church (the north door) is a slab without any inscription on it. It is commonly stated that the inscription is turned down, as it tells the sad tale of a clergyman being buried there, who was hanged for making base coin and issuing it.

A "sad tale" indeed, if true. The story of a clergyman turned counterfeiter and dying a felon's death. But what of the rest of the tale, what the motive for such a crime? The *Almanack* does not say; it tells only so much and as the compiler briefly records the story he apologises for its improbability—*it is commonly stated*, he writes, and with this disclaimer exonerates himself.

The story also found its way into Captain J. H. Lawrence-Archer's *Monumental Inscriptions of the British West Indies*, published in 1875; but here also the compiler is doubtful of its authenticity.

The Case of the Counterfeit Doubloons

"In front of the principal entrance by the north transept [of the Kingston Parish Church] is a large black marble slab, worn by feet, and without an inscription," he writes. "The story is, that it is 'turned on its face, to conceal the epitaph of an early rector of the parish, who was hanged, for coining counterfeit doubloons in the vestry. It is said he was discovered, in consequence of having issued one from his mint, before it was quite cold.' The story is most improbable."

But why was the story so improbable? Lawrence-Archer seems to have been a confirmed sceptic. He cast similar doubt on the circumstances of Lewis Galdy's providential escape at the time of the 1692 earthquake at Port Royal, although the testimony was clearly before his eyes, carved on the tombstone. And yet here, in one particular, his scepticism was justified, for the clergyman's connection with the tombstone was to prove in fact a fanciful fabrication of Time, the good Collector. Frank Cundall, one of the island's most industrious historians, in his *Historic Jamaica*, published in 1915, records that the question was finally settled in 1885 when the slab was raised and turned and the inscription, so long a mystery, at last revealed. The revelation proved an anticlimax; however, it answered one question, but conjured another in its place which has never been resolved, for the monument was found to be inscribed to the memory—not of a minister—but of a merchant of the city of Kingston, a certain James Ramadge who died in the year 1755, aged thirty-three years. Why the stone was placed face downwards remains unknown to this day.

So at last the footworn monument had given up its secret and Time had enjoyed his joke: beneath its shelter rested the remains of a merchant, not the clergyman around whose life had been woven a strange sad tale. Now that the story's connection with the stone was severed did that discredit the whole story, or was there indeed a faint pattern of truth somewhere in the confused fabric?

The story of *The Scarlet Letter* goes into legend, wrote the author. To legend also was consigned the story of the counterfeiting clergyman. But this was in defiance of evidence not easily set aside. As far back as 1801, the *St. Jago de la Vega Gazette*—an early Jamaican newspaper, founded in 1756—carried in its issue of 19th December this dispassionate notice:

A number of counterfeit Doubloons and Eight-Dollar pieces are now in circulation. The inscription on the face is Carol's 3d., date 1761. The face does not by any means resemble any effigy given of him or any coins issued by Spanish Government during his reign. It is a perfect copy of the head of Ferdinand the 6th, which appears on the doubloons issued by him ten years before the accession of Charles the 3rd to the throne. The pieces now in circulation are said to have been coined by a Reverend Mr. Smith, who suffered for the crime many years ago on the Kingston Parade.

An important early version of the story this, and one which seems to have been largely neglected. Lacking the romantic interest and unfettered by the myth of the plain stone slab, it also furnishes many details of value, including a vital clue—the clergyman's name: *a Reverend Mr. Smith.*

Frank Cundall recognised the importance of this account and tried to follow up the lead it gave. He discovered that a *Rev. Hadden Smith* was curate of the Kingston Parish Church in 1766. Can this have been the counterfeiter, he asks? But there he left the matter.

A Register of Marriages for the parish of Kingston for the years 1753 to 1814, in the Jamaica Archives, does show in fact that the Rev. Haddon Smith (as he himself spelt the name) acted as curate between September 1765 and July 1766. In those ten months he officiated at the marriage ceremonies of some twenty-six couples, including merchants, gentlemen, esquires. He married a planter of St. Andrew, a silversmith of Kingston, a "practitioner in physick and Chirurgery," a free Negro man named Thomas, a mariner, mill-wright, cordwainer, printer and perukemaker. He signed each page of the Register with a bold, clear hand, a sloping rather *pretty* hand, the hand of a . . . counterfeiter?

No. At any rate, not of the clergyman-counterfeiter who was hanged for his crime on the Kingston Parade, because six years later I found Haddon Smith in America, alive and well. As it happened, he was also in some hot water, but not from coining base doubloons. E. Merton Coulter in his *Georgia: A Short History*, (1947 Edition), writing about the American Declaration of Independence in 1776, records that: "The Rev. Haddon Smith, rector of Christ Church in Savannah, had the previous year refused to observe the fast ordered by the Continental Congress, and to add to his contumely, he made slighting remarks about the Provincial Congress. For this rebellion against rebellion he was at once published as a public enemy, and a vigilance committee ordered that he desist from further preaching."

So Cundall's question was answered and the name of Haddon Smith cleared of the crime of counterfeiting imputed to him. But there was in fact no need to guess at the identity of the counterfeiter. The unimpeachable documentary evidence of the man, his crime and punishment, were there to be found amidst the original records, safely preserved in the country's Archives.

And now with Haddon Smith out of the picture, my search for the "unfortunate clergyman" continued. It moved rapidly to its conclusion when I found traces of another Reverend Mr. Smith—a Francis Smith—in a Register of Baptisms, Marriages and Burials for St. Catherine. In this volume I discovered entries for the old parish of St. Dorothy for the period 1772 to 1775—"taken from the manuscript of the Rev. Francis Smith."

From this clue the search led logically to the records of the Grand Court, to the series known as *Pleas of the Crown* where, among the cases tried in the Surrey Assizes in April 1775, I came at last upon that of the counterfeiting clergyman—the case of *The King agst. the Reverend Francis Smith, Guilty.*

"Be it Remembered," begins the stern and solemn record, "Unto this Court it stands presented . . . that the Reverend Francis Smith late of the parish of Saint Dorothy in the County of Middlesex in the Island of Jamaica Clerk after the first day of January which was in the Year of our Lord one thousand seven hundred and seventy four, to wit, on the thirteenth day of ffebruary . . . did Import and cause and procure to be imported into the Town of Kingston . . . Forty four certain false base forged and counterfeit gold Monies and Coins each resembling and like to a portugal piece of Gold Coin called a half Johannes which half Johannes is a Coin of a foreign Realm to wit of the Kingdom of Portugal and then was and now is current in this Island And thirty one certain false base forged and counterfeit gold Monies and Coins each resembling and like to a piece of Spanish Gold Coin commonly called a milled Doubloon and sixteen certain false base forged and counterfeit gold Monies and Coins each resembling and like to a piece of Spanish gold Coin commonly called a milled two pistole piece which milled Doubloon and milled two pistole piece are Coins of a foreign Realm to wit of the Kingdom of Spain and then were and now are taken and received in this Island by general Consent knowing the said Monies and Coins . . . to be false base forged and counterfeit Against the form of an Act of the Lieutenant Governor Council and Afsembly of this Island in such Case made and provided And against the peace of our said Sovereign Lord the King his Crown and Dignity . . ."

Thus the charge, thrice repeated in the stern and solemn document.

Brought to the bar of the court and asked how he would acquit himself of the felony charged against him, Smith pleaded not guilty; but the jury trial which followed found otherwise. Asked if he knew or had anything to say for himself why the court should not award execution upon the verdict returned, the unhappy man repeated his plea of innocence, but the plea was rejected. The sentence: that he be "Hanged by his Neck until he be Dead."

The Case of the Counterfeit Doubloons

Was the Rev. Francis Smith hanged? I have no clear proof of this, but other surviving documentary evidence strongly suggests that he was. The month following his trial—on the 24th of May—he was buried, by the Rev. Thomas Coxeter, Rector of Kingston; not under a plain slate slab in the churchyard, but (according to the Parish Register) in the New Ground, under a White Pall, for the use of which someone (who could it have been?) paid the fee of £1. The cause of death is not given.

Also, in the Kingston *Vestry Accounts*, under date 1st September, 1775, appears this sinister entry: *Thos. Brown, for Gallows*, £5.17.6—the closing account, perhaps, of the strange case of the Counterfeit Doubloons.

The death of Three-fingered Jack

Three-fingered Jack

Beat big drum—wave fine flag:
Bring good news to Kingston Town, O!
No fear Jack's Obi-bag—
Quashee knock him down, O!

—*Jamaican folk-song*

IN THE FOLK-LORE of most countries there is the legend of
a hero, braver and stronger than his fellows, and invulnerable,
or nearly so. Jamaica is no exception. Across the stage of the
late eighteenth century moves the hero of Jamaican song and
story, the notorious Three-fingered Jack, whose life and
exploits, real enough at the time, have become legendary.

Writers of the period saw him in different lights: some, as
the bravest and strongest man in the world; others as "a
bold and daring defender of the rights of man." But Jack was

other things as well. To the majority of people who mattered during his lifetime he was an outlaw with a price on his head, a bandit and murderer who terrorised the island and defied the civil and military authorities for more than two years.

With the probable exception of Columbus, no other person connected with Jamaica has been the subject of as many publications as Jack Mansong, to give him his real name. The fantastic nature of his career leant itself to dramatisation, and devotees of "pantomimical drama" were not slow in seeing in the story good material for their craft. One play in particular, "invented by Mr. Fawcett, and got up under the direction of Mr. Farley," was performed with unbounded applause at the Theatre Royal, Haymarket, London, the published version running to many editions.

The earliest known account of Three-fingered Jack is given in a *Tretise on Sugar* by Doctor Benjamin Moseley, published in London in 1799. In the following year a work appeared dealing specially with the outlaw in the form of a series of *Letters* from a resident in Jamaica to his friend in England. Most other accounts are closely based on these two.

The story is that Jack's parents, Makro and Amri, were treacherously transported from Africa to Jamaica and sold as slaves by a Captain Henry Harrop whose life they had previously saved.

Harrop is described as ambitious, servile and, to aid his schemes, deceitful. "He had a smooth tongue, which gained him the good will of all. Artful and cunning, he could disguise the sentiments of his heart with the greatest ease, and his father, who bore the best character in the Island of Jamaica, whose humanity was daily praised by everyone, thought him a good and virtuous youth."

The elder Harrop was born in London, but a near relation having left him a small plantation in Jamaica, he came out to the island at the age of twenty-one to take it over. He was never of a very robust constitution and died a comparatively young man. His wife had predeceased him by many years. Henry was twenty-two at the time of his father's death and being an only son fell heir to a tolerably good estate. The story further relates that about this time a revolt of Coromantee slaves broke out in the island. Harrop is said to have been chiefly instrumental in bringing the ringleaders to justice, and one of the first, when order was restored, to see the need for speedy replacements of slaves on the plantations and the profit to be made from supplying them. He sold his property and with the proceeds fitted out two vessels for the African slave trade. The venture was a success and in two trips he recovered his capital outlay.

It was on a later voyage to the West Coast that Jack's parents had the misfortune of encountering Harrop and of saving him from drowning. He repaid them with treachery and murder, but in doing so signed his own death warrant, although he could not have guessed it at the time.

Not even his well-tested methods succeeded in breaking Makro's fierce spirit, and the latter died on the voyage to Jamaica after receiving five hundred lashes, refusing submission to the last. Amri, his wife, survived the crossing and on arrival at Morant Bay was sold as a slave to a Mr. Mornton of Maroon Town.

Her only thought now was of revenge, but there was little that she herself could do. When, three months later, however, her boy child Jack was born she instantly saw in him the means of vengeance for which she yearned. She reared him as well and carefully as conditions permitted, nurturing in his young breast the seeds of hatred and rebellion that flourished in hers.

Jack grew to an early, vigorous manhood, and gave every promise of fulfilling his mother's best hopes of him. The writer of the *Letters* has left us a vivid picture of the youthful Mansong. He describes him as "of the most manly growth, nearly seven feet in height, and amazingly robust; bred up to hardihood, his limbs were well shapen and athletic; he could endure the most laborious toil, and would with ease perform the office of any two negroes within the plantation. His face was rather long; his eyes black and fierce; his nose was not like the generality of blacks, squat and flat, but rather aquiline, and his skin remarkably clear. He discovered a great deal of expression in his countenance, and a very look of reproach from him would strike terror to his fellow-slaves."

He had readily absorbed his mother's teaching and, we are told, his dream of revenge became an obsession and "a balm at heart, which checked the corroding anguish of his daily toil." His first attempt to redress his wrongs, however, was rash and ill-timed. It was precipitated by his discovery that the hated Captain Harrop was staying at the very plantation to which he belonged. Jack tried to stir up the other slaves to revolt, but the effort failed. They lacked the motive and the cue for passion that he had. He was captured and tried for his life. The verdict, of course, was death—a peculiarly brutal death, if we may credit the writer of the *Letters* who says: "he was to be slung up by his waist, forty feet from the ground, to a gallows, exposed to the sun's burning heat and to those noxious insects of the West-Indies, that infect the body even to putridity, for three days, receiving no sustenance; on the fourth he was to be taken down, and the soles of his feet seared, and under the arm-pits, then to receive five hundred lashes, have his heart and entrails burnt before him, to be quartered, and his quarters to be hung in four several parts of the Island, to strike terror to the slaves."

But the night before his execution Jack broke out of prison, killed the two soldiers guarding him and escaped. He decided to make for the mountains—the refuge always of the outcast and the rebel—but first he went back to the plantation to say good-bye to Amri, then making his way cautiously to the great house surprised Harrop asleep. Knocking him senseless Jack flung the limp form over his shoulders with ease and was away into the mountains before the dead soldiers were discovered and the alarm given.

Jack took refuge in a cave near Mount Lebanus in St. Thomas-in-the-East where he decided to lie low until the hue and cry which followed his escape had died down. Harrop, who knew he had little else to expect at the outlaw's hands but death, pleaded nevertheless for his life. Jack had in fact decided not to kill him; he would need someone to cook and tend to his few wants, and what better revenge could he wish than to see his late master work as he had been made to work and to keep him chained to the wall of his cave as one would a beast of prey. It was here, after Mansong's death, that Harrop was eventually discovered . . . but, too late. The Fairburn edition of Three-fingered Jack is "embellished" with four crude coloured engravings, one of which shows the ghastly remains of a man chained hand and foot to the wall of a cave; the victim's skin is drawn tightly over the bones, the stomach is a gaping hole, the eyes hollow sockets: crudely drawn, but eloquent—the fate of Captain Henry Harrop.

Jack had carried off the cartridge boxes and muskets of the two soldiers, as well as a cutlass picked up at the plantation the night he escaped. Thus armed he was a formidable foe, but this was not enough for him. He wanted something more, something that would render him invulnerable!

In the neighbourhood of Mount Lebanus lived an obeah-man named Bashra, wrinkled and deformed. He had contracted the disease known as yaws when a younger man, and, as was the custom at the time, had been turned off the plantation to which he belonged and left to survive as best he might in the mountains. The disease had run its dreadful course and had transformed him into a hideous misshapen thing. So disabled was he that "snails drew their slimy trail upon his shrivelled feet, and lizards and vipers filled the air of his hut with foul uncleanliness."

He had taken up the ancient African practice of witchcraft known as *Obeah* (or *Obi*) as a means of livelihood and made a good business of it. His small hut, cunningly hidden by the thick foliage and interwoven trees, was the frequent resort of robbers and runaways who came to him for obeah spells and talismans to protect them from the weapons of their enemies.

To Bashra also came Three-fingered Jack with his request. Bashra was sympathetic. He agreed to arm him with the strongest obeah of which his craft was capable. With it Jack would be safe. Nothing could harm him, he said, nothing, nothing . . . except perhaps the white man's magic—that which they called Christianity.

Christianity: the one weak link in his magic armour, the Achilles' heel of his defence. Jack took the obeah prepared for him by Bashra and left, but he never forgot the other's words.

"I saw the Obi of the famous Negro robber Three-fingered Jack," writes Dr. Moseley; "the Maroons who slew him brought it to me. His Obi consisted of the end of a goat's horn, filled with a compound of grave dirt, ashes, the blood of a black cat, and human fat; all mixed into a kind of paste. A cat's foot, a dried toad, a pig's tail, a slip of virginal parchment of kid's skin, with characters marked in blood on it, were also in his Obian bag.

"These, with a keen sabre, and two guns like Robinson Crusoe were all his Obi; with which, and his courage in descending into the plains and plundering to supply his wants, and his skill in retreating into difficult fastnesses, among the mountains, commanding the only access to them, where none dared to follow him, he terrified the inhabitants, and set the civil power, and the neighbouring militia of that island, at defiance for nearly two years.

"He had neither accomplice, nor associate. There were a few runaway Negroes in the woods near Mount Lebanus, the place of his retreat; but he had crossed their foreheads with some of the magic in his horn, and they could not betray him. But he trusted no one. He scorned assistance. He robbed alone; fought all his battles alone; and always killed his pursuers."

. . . all his pursuers, but one, a Maroon named Quashee, who had trailed Jack once to his lair while the latter was returning from a secret visit to his mother, and attacked him. That fight cost Jack two of his fingers and gave him at the same time the nickname for which he was to become so famous, while Quashee had barely escaped with his life.

Besides his retreat at Mount Lebanus, Jack also used the

Cambridge Hill and Cane River Caves as hideouts. Many are the stories told of his amazing strength. It is said that he could sever a horse's head with one stroke of his cutlass. Bloody and merciless as he was, it is recorded to his credit that he never harmed a woman. The story is told that on one of his sorties he came on the wife of a British soldier who asked him to escort her along the road to Moore Town as a protection from the dreaded Three-fingered Jack! He agreed, and together they made their way up the road through the Blue Mountains that overlooks Nanny Town, and it was not till near the end of the journey that they parted company. The woman offered to reward Jack for accompanying her, but, smiling wryly, he showed her his mutilated hand and said,

"Now you see who I am. Put up your money and go your way in safety!"

It is odd that although Jack was never known to abuse a woman or disturb one lady's happiness, every conjugal mishap was laid at his door. The fact is that girls at that time were often married to much older men than themselves, with the result that many matches proved unsuccessful. Heaven knows Jack had sins enough of his own to carry without taking on the sins of others, still whenever a marriage failed there was a loud outcry against him as it was believed that he had used his malefic spell of *tying the point* on the wedding day!

It is the writer of the *Letters* who gives us a vivid picture of the general effect the outlaw had on the social life of the time. "And so it is with everybody in the Island," he writes; "go wherever I will, the name of Jack is perpetually buzzed in my ears. If I meet a friend in the street, it is no longer 'How d'ye do?' but 'Well, what news of Jack?' If any of my neighbours, calling his servant, says: 'Jack, come here,' I start and stare about, in expectation of seeing the three-fingered one make his appearance. Nay, there is not a *thing* called Jack, whether a smoke-jack, a boot-jack, or any other jack, but acts as a spell upon my senses and sets me on the fret at the bare mention of it."

As time went on Jack's forays became more daring and

alarming. He was in himself a terrifying menace, while to the imminent danger of foreign invasion he added the constant risk of revolt among the slaves in the eastern part of the island. All efforts to capture him had failed, meanwhile his depredations increased in range and success. Three-fingered Jack had become the terror of Jamaica!

On the 8th December, 1780, the House of Assembly forwarded a resolution to the Governor, Colonel John Dalling, requesting him to issue His Majesty's Royal Proclamation offering a reward of £100 for Jack's capture. A week later the Proclamation was published. A fortnight later the House resolved that,

> . . . over and above the reward of One hundred pounds offered by His Majesty's Proclamation the further reward of FREEDOM shall be given to any slave that shall take or kill the said Three-fingered Jack.

By the 13th January, 1781, the House of Assembly had carried the reward for Jack's capture to £300!

Three-fingered Jack was now at the peak of his career, a dreaded outlaw with a high price on his head. But the sands were running out, as he knew some day they must, and the end was near, nearer than he could have guessed.

Tempted by the reward Quashee determined to pit himself against the three-fingered one a second time. On this occasion he was accompanied by another Maroon named Sam, as well as a party of his townsmen from Scott's Hall. Before setting out he had himself baptised and his name changed to James Reeder. The Whiteman's Magic, he argued, might prove stronger than Jack's Obi.

It did.

For three weeks the party crept about the woods blockading the deepest recesses of the most inaccessible part of the island where Jack had elected to live, but without any success. Tired of this long drawn out action, Reeder and Sam resolved to search for the outlaw's retreat and take it by storm. For this the smaller the number the better the chance of success, so taking a young boy, described as "a proper spirit, and a good shot," they parted company with the rest of the group.

Success was almost immediate. They spotted footprints which they followed. Soon they caught sight of smoke in the distance and made their way towards it. So stealthy was their approach, however, that they came on Jack before he was aware of them. He was sitting at the mouth of his cave roasting plantains by a little fire on the ground.

He leapt to his feet at sight of the intruders, a savage growl escaping from his enormous chest as he recognised the leader. He rolled his black eyes ominously and held up his mutilated hand for the trio to see. "This was a scene," writes Dr. Moseley, "not where ordinary actors had a common part to play. Here was the stage on which two of the stoutest hearts, that were ever hooped with ribs, began their bloody struggle."

"You are brave to come again, Quashee," Jack cried, "but this time it will cost you your life!"

But instead of cowering, the Maroon laughed in Jack's face.

"I am not *Quashee* any longer," he said, "my name is James Reeder. I am christened now, and your obeah can no longer harm me!"

Jack staggered backwards, his eyes dilated with horror at the other's words. Suddenly it seemed that the years had rolled back and he was in the hut of Bashra the obeahman, listening again to the awful prophecy which, in all that intervening time, had lain like dust upon his thoughts.

At his feet the two rifles lay, forgotten, his cutlass hung loosely in his hand. Suddenly his nerve failed him; he wheeled, dived into the cave and threw himself down a precipice at the back.

As he turned Sam shot him in the shoulder, but Reeder's gun misfired. Throwing aside the useless weapon, he darted into the cave and plunged headlong down the precipice after Jack. The descent was about thirty feet and almost perpendicular, but both men managed to keep hold of their cutlasses in the fall.

Three-fingered Jack

The small boy who had been warned to stay out of harm's way, now reached the top of the precipice and, as the two men duelled violently on the narrow ledge of rock on to which they had fallen, took careful aim and shot Jack in the stomach.

Sam took a safer but more circuitous route to the scene of battle only to find on arrival that both men had plunged down yet another precipice, losing their cutlasses in the fall. Abandoning his weapon also he slid quickly down the hillside, arriving on the scene just in time for by now Jack, although in mortal agony, had Reeder by the throat in a giant's grasp, the latter being almost defenceless as his right arm had been nearly severed in the fight. With a large rock Sam knocked Jack senseless and, as he lay unconscious, he and Reeder finished the job by battering out his brains with smaller stones.

The boy soon made his way down to them, bringing a cutlass with which they cut off the head and huge three-fingered hand from the blood-soaked body. They then set off for Morant Bay with their good news and grisly trophies which they placed in a pail of rum, the better to preserve them. Word spread rapidly and soon they were joined by hundreds of their fellows, no longer afraid of Jack's obeah, blowing their shells and horns and firing their guns as the procession started on the long trek to Kingston and thence to Spanish Town to claim the rewards offered by the Royal Proclamation and the Jamaica House of Assembly.

Nor did the Government's gratitude end with these rewards. Jack's captor was voted a pension which, according to the records of *Revenue and Expenditure*, was still being paid as late as 1840 (it probably continued beyond this date) almost sixty years after the event.

Although more than a century and a half have gone by, the memory of Jack still lives. His name is perpetuated in a spring in St. Thomas, his story has passed into the island's folklore, while in the neighbourhood of Mount Lebanus there are people who still speak of the day the procession passed along Cedar Valley bearing the head and three-fingered hand of Jack Mansong, the terror of Jamaica.

The Shark Papers

THIS IS the story not so much of people, as of a packet of documents now known the world over as "The Shark Papers"—one of the strangest stories of all time.

It centres around a lawsuit tried in the Jamaica Court of Vice-Admiralty some one hundred and sixty-five years ago, a suit which, involving as it did the legality of a prize taken in Caribbean waters by a British warship, was in itself neither novel nor very important, but as an instance of providential intervention, as an example of the truth of the saying that fact is often stranger than fiction, the case of "The Shark Papers" is without peer.

To trace the events of this remarkable narrative we must think back to the Port of Baltimore, Maryland, on a July morning in the year 1799, when a certain brig named *Nancy* cleared for the long voyage to Curaçao in the Dutch West Indies.

A vessel of some 125 tons, *Nancy* was one of a fleet of more than forty ships employed by the firm of Deverhagen, Groverman & Co., of Baltimore, trading between that port, Curaçao and Haiti. The cargoes which consisted chiefly of German goods were usually shipped to Curaçao for sale, the vessels calling at Haiti on the homeward voyage for coffee.

The *Nancy* left Baltimore with Thomas Briggs (an American, born in Dighton, Massachusetts) as master; her crew, including officers, numbered seven and was made up mostly of Danes and Swedes. Her cargo, a varied one, consisted mainly of provisions, lumber and dry goods, including such items as soap, candles, prunes, pickled fish and thirty-seven cases of claret.

The brig had done the trip before, but this was to be the most eventful. This was, in fact, to be her last. It was near the end of the voyage when falling to leeward "in consequence of wind and current" as it was claimed, Briggs decided to put in at Aruba, some fifty miles distant from Curaçao.

It is possible that the vessel did fall to leeward for the reason given. This often happened. But not infrequently also it was a cunningly executed manœuvre in order to have an excuse for being off course. The French Revolutionary struggles were at their height and Great Britain was at war with France, Spain and the Netherlands. The Caribbean was a seething cauldron of conflict in which neutral ports such as Aruba had a significant role to play, affording a haven to ships of all nations and doing a rip-roaring business of supplying them with arms and false papers, as well as clearing cargoes intended for prohibited ports.

From Aruba Briggs went to Curaçao by drogher, rejoining his vessel some time later, accompanied by a Mr. Christopher Schultze, agent for Deverhagen & Co., and an important figure in the firm: one of the fleet had been named in his honour and he had a brother highly placed in the Baltimore head office.

Mr. Schultze seems to have found everything about the brig in proper order, or, perhaps we should say, to his satisfaction, and *Nancy* cleared port without more delay on the return leg of her journey. She was making the best of her way to Port-au-Prince when she carried away her main-topmast. Cursing his bad luck, Captain Briggs was forced to steer for the Ile-à-Vache, a small island off the south coast of Haiti, as the nearest place in which to refit. As it happened, he never made port.

On 28th August *Nancy* was sighted by H.M.S. *Sparrow*, a British cutter commanded by Hugh Whylie, which immediately gave chase. Briggs clapped on every shred of canvas and tried to run for it, but in her disabled state his vessel was no match for the swift cutter. The warship signalled with a gun to stop and Briggs obeyed. During the chase he had gone below to his cabin for a short time, but now he was back on deck. His eyes narrowed with hate as he watched the British prize crew rowing towards his vessel and the hands clasped behind his back showed taut white skin at the knuckles, but he was strangely calm and around the corners of his lips lurked the ghost of a smile . . . for Captain Thomas Briggs was ready to meet his captors.

Whylie lost no time in taking over the *Nancy*, sealing up her papers and sending her in to Port Royal in the company of another prize, a Spanish schooner, which he had taken earlier.

On 9th September, 1799, a suit for salvage was brought in the Court of Vice-Admiralty in Kingston by the Advocate-General George Crawford Ricketts, on behalf of Hugh Whylie, Commander of His Majesty's Cutter *Sparrow*, his officers, seamen, marines and mariners, against "A Certain Brig or Vessel called the Nancy, her Guns Tackle furniture Ammunition and Apparel and the Goods Wares Merchandise Specie and Effects on board her taken and Seized as property of some person or persons being Enemies of our Sovereign

Lord the King and good and lawful prize on the high Seas and within the Jurisdiction of this Court."

Five days after the filing of the salvage suit a claim for dismissal, with costs, was entered by Briggs backed by affidavits in which, as events were to show, he and Schultze perjured themselves freely.

The case came on for trial. Briggs's claim was ably conducted. The suit seemed to be going in his favour when events took a fantastic turn with the arrival in Kingston of Acting Lieutenant Michael Fitton of H.M.S. *Ferret*, a tender of *Abergavenny* the flagship at Port Royal.

Proceedings came to a temporary halt for Lieutenant Fitton had important information to deliver touching the case, as well as an odd-looking bundle of documents tied with a string, which he lodged with one of the Surrogates of the Court. This done, proceedings were resumed, but not as before, for what had been a dull, ordinary lawsuit, had suddenly become one of the most exciting and extraordinary as the story of the odd-looking bundle of documents, now known as "The Shark Papers," slowly unravelled itself.

This story began a very short time before, towards the end of August, while Fitton in the *Ferret* and Whylie in H.M.S. *Sparrow* were cruising in company off Santo Domingo.

Both vessels had gone out in the hope of earning a share of the prizes which were constantly being taken by the warships in the neighbourhood and during their cruise were accidentally separated for a short time. They sighted each other again on the morning of the 30th, and Fitton invited Whylie by signal to come aboard his ship for breakfast. It was while awaiting his arrival that the watch on the *Ferret* hailed the deck to say there was a strange object floating off the port beam. It turned out to be a dead bullock, half-eaten by sharks which were in fact still feeding on the carcass as it floated near the warship. Fitton ordered it taken in tow alongside for he had noticed an unusually large shark swimming nearby which he hoped to catch.

Michael Fitton, as events will show, was an uncommonly lucky fisherman. The shark was caught and hoisted safely on deck. Some of the crew were detailed to separate and clean the jaws and others to cut open the maw in which, to their astonishment, they found *a bundle of papers tied up with a string*. Fitton looked them over quickly, noticing a letter of recent date from Curaçao. An examination of the remaining documents proved most interesting for they turned out to be the papers of some ship—perhaps one of the prizes recently taken in those waters—and no doubt thrown overboard by her master at the time of capture, but now restored to custody in this remarkable way!

Fitton gave orders for the documents to be carefully opened and dried on deck as he went to greet Whylie, arrived in good time for their breakfast appointment, smiling inwardly to think how good a fish story he had to tell his guest!

The commander of the *Sparrow*, however, had stories of his own to tell and lost no time in doing so. He was in good humour and talked animatedly about his exploits during their short separation. His luck had been fair, he had taken a couple of quite profitable prizes including an American brig named *Nancy*, which he had sent into Kingston Harbour in company of another prize, a Spanish schooner captured earlier.

Fitton started at the other's information. "The *Nancy*, did you say?" he asked. "How very interesting. I think I have her papers!"

"That's impossible," Whylie said. "I sealed them up myself after the capture and sent them in with her."

"Those, I'm afraid, must have been false ones," answered Michael Fitton, rising, "for if you will come on deck with me I'll show you a bundle of ship's papers recovered only a short time ago from the stomach of a shark which, I think, belongs to your *Nancy* brig!"

Fitton of course, was right. Those papers, which he later handed in to the Vice-Admiralty Court at the crucial moment in the case, together with others of a highly incriminating nature later discovered on board the vessel concealed in the captain's cabin "so hard drove in that it was with difficulty they could be taken out," as well as a book found hidden in a cask of salt-fish, led to the condemnation on 25th November, 1799, of the brig and her cargo as good and lawful prize on the high seas.

Discovered among "The Shark Papers" were letters of instruction from Deverhagen & Co. to Schultze as to the course of action he should take in case of certain eventualities. The following excerpts are clear evidence of the firm's illegal transactions:

> Mr. C. Schultze will take his passage in the schooner *Triumph* for Curaçao, and, after his arrival there, will put his cargo in Stores, dismiss the crew, and send back the Captain, with all the papers; he will get Dutch papers for the vessel, and cause himself to be naturalised a Dutch citizen . . .

> Mr. Dubourg ought to be more prudent in case such letters be miscarried; great and many difficulties would arise of such a negligence . . .

And this revealing item:

> We shall thank you, and you will oblige us to be more silent of our business: nobody gains to be informed of our transactions, and give us only here trouble and town talk . . .

Nancy was not the only vessel of the fleet which met disaster. In the correspondence is a reference to the capture of the *Governor Lauffer* by His Majesty's brig *Diligent* and of the *Highlander* which was taken into Guadeloupe. Elsewhere we read, "The *Coquette* is lost; at least, nothing has been heard of her. The *Trent* foundered two days after she left Curaçao . . ."

"The Shark Papers," together with Lieutenant Fitton's affidavit describing how they came into his hands, were kept on file in the Vice-Admiralty Court's archives until 1890 when they were passed to the Institute of Jamaica for display in the History Gallery where they have attracted considerable attention.

The surviving Court records now in the Jamaica Archives, Spanish Town, include the answers of both Briggs and Schultze to the *Preparatory Examination*, in which they deposed on oath that "no papers whatever were burnt torn *thrown overboard* destroyed cancelled concealed or attempted so to be . . . that all the Papers on Board said Brig were entirely true and fair."

Among these records are also a number of papers found on board the brig, but they are not of great interest as few refer to *Nancy* herself but to various other vessels in which Schultze and his principals at Baltimore were interested.

Formerly in the Royal United Service Museum, London, but now in the Institute of Jamaica, are the jaws of the shark which swallowed the papers, together with a box containing yet more of the documents found on *Nancy*, probably those which were not required as evidence in the salvage suit. They are mostly in French and date from about the last quarter of the eighteenth century.

Before their removal to London, the jaws of the shark adorned for a short time the shore near the old court house at the corner of Hanover and Harbour Streets, Kingston, fittingly inscribed:

LIEUT. FITTON RECOMMENDS THESE JAWS FOR A COLLAR FOR NEUTRALS TO SWEAR THROUGH

Fitton, as we have seen, was blessed with a rare faculty for catching odd fish. The story is told that when on his first ship, the *Vestal*, Captain George Keppel, on the 10th September, 1780, while chasing the *Mercury* packet having on board Henry Laurens, late President of Congress, on his way to Holland as minister plenipotentiary of the American Colonies, then in revolt, in furtherance of secret negotiations for a commercial treaty which had been some time in progress, Fitton, being on the foretopgallant yard, hailed the deck to say that a man was overboard from the enemy. The object was recovered and found to be a bag of papers, not weighted sufficiently to sink it. On examination these papers were found to compromise the Dutch Government and led to the imprisonment of Laurens in the Tower of London and a declaration of war against Holland a few months afterwards!

Michael Scott, the author of *Tom Cringle's Log* (1833), drew inspiration from the strange case of "The Shark Papers" for a yarn told in his other book about the island *The Cruise of the Midge* (published the following year) in which *Nancy* is represented as the Yankee brig *Alconda* and Captain Briggs by the gaunt, tobacco-chewing Jonathan who, much as his real-life counterpart might have done, swung out of court when the trial was over, exclaiming, amidst a shower of tobacco juice:

"Pretty considerably damned and con-damned, and all by a bloody sharkfish. If this ben't, by G—, the most active and unnatural piece of cruelty—may I be physicked all my natural days with hot oil and fish-hooks!"

One more short chapter, recorded by DeValda in his book *Full Measure* (1933), was added to the story of "The Shark Papers" at the time of the Kingston earthquake of 1907. Soon after the disaster bands of looters began to roam the city. Luckily the authorities managed to deal promptly and effectively with them. DeValda recalls searching one "doubtful individual" and finding a bundle of documents for which he could not account. This turned out to be "The Shark Papers"! He later returned them to the Institute from which they had been stolen.

Acknowledgements

Thanks are due to the following for permission to use the illustrations reproduced in this book: illustrations to chapters 1, 5, 9, 10, The Royal Commonwealth Society; chapters 3, 4, 7, 8, The Institute of Jamaica; chapter 2, The Trustees of the British Museum; chapter 6, the Jamaican Archives.